JOSEPH
makes me
think of
JESUS

JOSEPH
makes me think of
JESUS

William MacDonald

GOSPEL FOLIO PRESS
P. O. Box 2041, Grand Rapids MI 49501-2041
Available in the UK from JOHN RITCHIE LTD.,
40 Beansburn, Kilmarnock, Scotland

Published by Gospel Folio Press
P. O. Box 2041, Grand Rapids, MI 49501-2041

ISBN 1-882701-69-0

All Scripture quotations are from the New King James Version unless otherwise indicated. New King James © 1979, 1980, 1982. Thomas Nelson Inc.,
Publisher

Cover design by J. B. Nicholson, Jr.

Printed in the United States of America

CONTENTS

INTRODUCTION

You would have liked Joseph. He was an outstanding fellow. In addition to a warm, winning personality, he had a "conscience live and keen" when it came to moral and ethical questions. Joseph was both loving and lovable. He was also handsome. Although he was not flawless, he was one of two men in the Old Testament of whom no fault or failure is recorded. The other was Daniel.

There are over one hundred correspondences between the life of Joseph and that of the Lord Jesus, so it is no wonder that our hearts are drawn to him. The Bible never says he was a type of Christ,[1] but the resemblance is undeniable. We can't read the story of his life without thinking of the Savior of the world. Joseph lived 2000 years before Jesus, and men who could not have conferred, of course, wrote their biographies, but the similarities are unmistakable. That becomes evident as we turn to the sacred record. It's not surprising that more space in Genesis is given to Joseph than to any other person.

Chapter One

JOSEPH'S EARLY LIFE

A root out of dry ground (Gen. 35:23-26)

When I say that Joseph was a root out of dry ground, I mean that his background was not promising. It was not likely that such a person would come from such an environment. His father, Jacob, had four wives and therefore all the troubles that polygamy engenders. One of Joseph's stepbrothers committed incest with one of his father's wives. Two of his stepbrothers were notoriously cruel, and another stepbrother got in trouble with a harlot. Today we would call that a dysfunctional family. But the grace of God triumphed over Joseph's heredity and environment, and he lived to make history for God.

The Lord Jesus was the true root out of dry ground

(Isa. 53:2). In His case, the dry ground was the nation of Israel. Its spiritual condition was not what it should have been for the arrival of the Messiah. He came like a tender plant growing up in a desert. Yet in spite of adverse circumstances, He too made good history for God. In fact, He is the pivotal person in God's majestic plan.

Shepherd (Gen. 37:2)

When we first meet Joseph, he was feeding his flock with his brothers. As he cared for animals that can be clueless and exasperating at times, he learned lessons that would serve him well in days to come: lessons of patience, tenderness, sympathy, and faithfulness.

Joseph foreshadows our Lord, the ideal Shepherd. A. W. Pink says,

> The figure suggests His watchful care, His unwearied devotion, His tender solicitude, His blessed patience, His protecting grace, and His matchless love in giving His life for the sheep.

We know Him as the Good Shepherd, the Great Shepherd, and the Chief Shepherd. But boys and girls in many homes prefer to call Him *Jesus, tender Shepherd,* when they pray to Him each evening.

Son of his father's love (Gen. 37:3)

Conventional wisdom tells us that parents should not play favorites with their children. But the hard fact of life is that many parents do have a favorite child, and Joseph's father Jacob was one of the many. He had a special love for his wife Rachel, and that love passed down to

Rachel's firstborn son, Joseph. No doubt, Joseph's sterling character also helped to endear him to his father. This special love reminds us of the love of the heavenly Father for His unique Son. Twice God opened heaven to announce publicly, *"This is My beloved Son, in whom I am well pleased"* (Mt. 3:17; 17:5). But we cannot say that God is guilty of favoritism. He has many children in addition to His unique Son. Every true believer is a child of God. The breathtaking truth is that He loves every one of them with the same love with which He loves the Lord Jesus (Jn. 17:23). The mutual love of Jacob and Joseph is one of the great themes of this saga. Jacob could not conceal his special affection for this stalwart son. Though separated for years, he never ceased to mourn for him. And Joseph reciprocated that love. In his prolonged separation, he never failed to inquire for his father.

So it is with the heavenly Joseph. Jesus said, *"Therefore My Father loves Me, because I lay down My life that I may take it again"* (Jn. 10:17). Repeatedly God calls the Lord Jesus *My beloved Son.* In Colossians 1:13, Paul calls our Lord *the Son of His love.*

Son of his father's old age (Gen. 37:3)

The reason given by the Scripture for the special love shown by Jacob to Joseph is that Joseph was born when his father was quite elderly. Jacob could have been in his eighties. He realized that his time on earth was limited, so there was special joy connected with the birth of a son at this stage of his life. Thus it was late in the history of

11

Israel (Jacob's God-given name) when Joseph was born. So with Christ: all hope seemed to be gone—until He came in *"the fullness of time"* (Gal. 4:4). We must be guarded in drawing an analogy with the Lord Jesus here. God, His Father, does not grow old. He never reaches old age. But since one of the names of God is the Ancient of Days (Dan. 7:9), we are safe in saying that Jesus is the Son of the Ancient of Days.[2]

A distinctive robe (Gen. 37:3)

Jacob gave Joseph a coat of many colors, an expression of special love for him. In a sense this set Joseph apart from his eleven brothers. It marked him out as different. People may argue that it was unwise for the father to do this, but the Holy Spirit would use it to point forward to another loved Son at whose death another robe would figure prominently.

The scene was Calvary, where the Lamb of God was nailed to a cross. The Roman soldiers laid claim to several items of His clothing, and divided them among themselves. But there was a seamless robe which couldn't be divided without destroying its usefulness. So they gambled for it. Pause here to marvel at Denney's reminder, "His was the greatest life ever lived on earth, and He left nothing but the clothes that He wore."

Joseph's brothers dipped his multicolored tunic in the blood of a young goat to deceive their father into thinking that Joseph had been slain. A strange coincidence that the Savior's robe should also be linked to His death.

I hope I'm not carrying typology too far if I suggest

that Jesus has a coat of many colors. First, a word of explanation. Clothing is sometimes used as a figure for character. For instance, *"Put on the new man which was created according to God, in righteousness and true holiness"* (Eph. 4:24). *"Be clothed with humility"* (1 Pet. 5:5). *"The fine linen is the righteous acts of the saints"* (Rev. 19:8). So I would suggest that the multi-colored garment of the Savior means the sum of all His glorious virtues: His wisdom, love, power, righteousness, holiness, grace, mercy, truth, and all His other perfections.

The appointed heir (1 Chron. 5:2b)

Reuben was Jacob's firstborn by Leah (1 Chron. 5:1) and thus should have inherited a double portion of his father's estate as well as headship of that tribe. But because he sinned by sleeping with his father's concubine, he lost the birthright and it was given to Joseph (1 Chron. 5:2b). When the land of Canaan was eventually divided among the tribes of Israel, Joseph received a double portion, one for his son Ephraim and one for Manasseh.

This is a faint foreshadowing of One who, as Firstborn (Rom. 8:29), is appointed to be Heir. Here it is not a matter of inheriting a few parcels of real estate, but all things (Heb. 1:2). It is nothing short of universal dominion.

Hated without a cause (Gen. 37:4)

If Joseph was such a splendid fellow, why did his brothers hate him? First of all, a family does not always appreciate one of its member's greatness. *"A prophet is not without honor except in his own country and in his own house"* (Mt. 13:57; see also Mt. 10:36). Second, Joseph's brothers were jealous of him, perhaps because of his coat of many colors and what it meant (Gen. 37:11; Acts 7:9). Then again, there was the dislike of the unlike. Joseph's righteous life was a rebuke to them and convicted them of their unrighteousness.

So it was in the experience of the Lord Jesus. He could say in the language of Psalm 69:8, *"I have become a stranger to My brothers, and an alien to My mother's children."* His brothers hated him without any valid reason. At one time they even thought He was deranged and tried to hustle him away (Mk. 3:21).

The religious leaders of Israel were also jealous of Him. They feared that everyone would believe on Him, and the Romans would crush their temple and nation (Jn. 11:48). It was because of envy that they delivered him up to Pilate (Mt. 27:18). As He Himself explained, *"Everyone practicing evil hates the light and does not come to the light, lest his deeds should be exposed"* (Jn. 3:20).

It is unimaginable that when the Creator-God came to this earth, His creatures should despise him. That the words *Jesus* and *was hated* should ever be spoken in the same breath is absolutely incongruous.

Dreams with a meaning (Gen. 37:5-11)
Twice Joseph dreamed that his family would bow to him, that he would reign over them. In the first dream, he saw sheaves of ripened grain bowing to his sheaf. The sheaves represented his brothers. In the second dream,

the solar system paid homage to him. The sun and moon personified his parents. The stars were his brothers. When he explained this dream, his father rebuked him and his brothers were livid with envy. Some might fault Joseph for revealing the dreams, but in the sovereign purposes of God, it was necessary that he do it. Otherwise, how could it be seen that Joseph's—and Christ's—exaltation was pre-planned by God, not a political accident?

His brothers said they would never bow to him, but circumstances later forced them to do it three times (Gen. 42:6; 43:28; 44:14), and finally they did it willingly (Gen. 50:18). In speaking to Joseph in chapters 42-50, they called themselves *"your servants"* at least fourteen times. How often they had to eat their words! Only God can say never.

Centuries later the Son of Man prophesied that He would return to earth as a conquering Monarch in power and great glory. In saying this, He implied that His people would pay homage to Him.

> *Then the sign of the Son of Man will appear in heaven, and then all the tribes of the earth will mourn, and they will see the Son of Man coming on the clouds of heaven with power and great glory* (Mt. 24:30).

> *Hereafter you will see the Son of Man sitting at the right hand of the Power, and coming in the clouds of heaven* (Mt. 26:64).

His people will be willing in the day of His power (see Ps. 110:3, KJV).

In his book, *A Fruitful Bough,*[3] Christopher Knapp

makes an interesting observation concerning the two dreams. The setting of the first is on earth (sheaves of grain). The locale of the second is the heavens (the sun, moon, and stars). Knapp suggests that this anticipates the time when

...at the name of Jesus every knee should bow, of those in heaven, and of those on earth, and of those under the earth, and that every tongue should confess that Jesus Christ is Lord, to the glory of God the Father (Phil. 2:10-11).

He also links the dreams with Ephesians 1:10:

...that in the dispensation of the fullness of the times He might gather together in one all things in Christ, both which are in heaven and which are on earth—in Him.

Something to think about (Gen. 37:11)

Joseph's father pondered the things that were happening. After Joseph revealed his dream, his father kept wondering about the foretold reign of his son. At the moment, it seemed very unlikely; but by a strange chain of circumstances it came to pass.

When we read this account, our minds quickly skip over to the mother of our Lord at the time of His birth. After the shepherds revealed that the Baby was the *"Savior, who is Christ the Lord,"* Mary *"kept all these things and pondered them in her heart."* That she, a humble Jewish maiden, should be the mother of the Messiah amazed her (Lk. 2:19). There was something about both these children's lives that made their parents think.

Sent by his father (Gen. 37:13)

His father sent Joseph on a special mission. After his brothers had gone to Shechem to find pasture for their sheep, Jacob sent Joseph to see how they were getting along. His obedient son responded instantly. His father said, "Go." He went. It was not a spying mission but an honest inquiry concerning their welfare and a routine business inspection of the livestock. Jacob's wealth was in his flocks.

The resemblance with the Lord Jesus is unmistakable. Over forty times in John's Gospel, He said that His Father sent Him (*e.g.,* Jn. 4:34; 8:42). Paul reminds us that God sent His Son in the fullness of time (Gal. 4:4) and John is clear in insisting that *"the Father has sent the Son as Savior of the world"* (1 Jn. 4:14). The Lord told the Jews that in order to do the works of God they must believe in Him whom He [the Father] sent (Jn. 6:29). The obedience of the Son shines out in His noble words, *"I have come— in the volume of the book it is written of Me—to do Your will, O God"* (Heb. 10:7). The Father called, *"Whom shall I send?"* The Son replied, *"Here I am. Send Me."*

Just as Joseph left the Valley of Hebron (meaning *fellowship*) to go to Shechem (a place of danger because two of his brothers had savaged the men there, Gen. 34:25-30), so the Lord left the peace of heaven to come down to this jungle of deceit and depravity. No one will ever know what it meant to the holy Son of God to step down from the realms of light into this scene of moral darkness. The more refined and godly a person is, the more he or she is revolted and repulsed by sin and filth.

17

Seeking the lost (Gen. 37:15)

When it says that a certain man found Joseph *"wandering in the field,"* it does not mean that he was aimless or lost. Rather it means that he had to look for his brothers where they were not supposed to be. They had drifted far. In that sense he was wandering. That is the way it was when Jesus came to the nation of Israel. Only a few, like Simeon and Anna, were awaiting His coming. The rest were spiritually unprepared for His advent.

The field is the world. Jesus "wander[ed] as a homeless stranger in the world His hands had made" (*James G. Deck*) seeking the lost sheep of the house of Israel who had wandered far from God.

A non-welcome (Gen. 37:18-20)

Instead of being pleased to see Joseph, his brothers were angry. Instead of receiving him graciously, courteously, and favorably, they taunted Him as an impractical dreamer. Perhaps they suspected him of coming to make them bow to him and feared he would tattle on them to their father. Some moderns do criticize him for tattling. In his defense it should be said that he was responsible to his father to give an accurate report concerning his brothers and the flocks. Since Jacob's wealth was measured in part by his animals, he wanted to know if they were healthy and multiplying. In addition, it has always been God's will that His people should not only refuse fellowship with the unfruitful works of darkness, but should reprove them (Eph. 5:11). Joseph could not lie concerning the behavior of his brothers. Is there a suggestion here that Jacob had reason to suspect them of unfaithfulness? A *"Greater than Joseph"* came from heaven's highest glory 2,000 years ago to seek and to save those who were lost. What kind of reception did He receive? The answer is given in John 1:11: *"He came to His own, and His own did not receive Him."* We don't get the full impact of this verse until we remember that it was their God whom they did not receive. It was the One who created them and on whom they depended for their life at any moment. The 'No vacancy" sign on the inn was a foreshadow of His non-welcome.

The plot to kill (Gen. 37:20)

The possibility that Joseph might have dominion over his brothers rankled them. They decided that the surest way to have his dreams thwarted would be to kill him and throw his body into a pit. Then they would concoct the lie that an animal had devoured him. What followed was a picture of what would happen to the Son of God at Calvary. They killed Joseph, in figure, if not in fact.

History repeated itself in the life of Jesus of Nazareth. The plots began soon after He was born: Herod sought His life. The religious rulers of Israel considered Him a threat so they repeatedly plotted His death (Mt.12:14; 26:3-4). Their attitude is accurately exposed in the parable of the wicked vinedressers (Mt. 21:33-46). When the owner of the vineyard (God) sent his servants (the prophets) to collect the income (a harvest of holiness and other spiritual fruit), the vinedressers (chief priests and Pharisees, v. 45) killed them. Finally, he sent his son (the

Lord Jesus), expecting them to respect him. But they said, *"This is the heir. Come, let us kill him and seize the inheritance"* (v. 38). In the parable of the minas (*"pounds"* KJV), they said, *"We will not have this Man to reign over us"* (Lk. 19:14).

Finally they arranged for a traitor to deliver Him for a civil and religious trial, for false witnesses to testify, and for a guilty sentence to be coerced. Never lose sight of the fact that the One they nailed to a cross of wood was the Creator and Upholder of the universe.

Change of plan (Gen. 37:21-22, 26-27)

Reuben urged his brothers not to kill Joseph, but to throw him into a pit, hoping he would escape and return to his father. Judah also argued against killing him but said that there would be no profit for them in simply throwing him into a pit. Why not make some quick cash by selling him to a passing caravan? Judah's covetous argument prevailed.

The Redeemer also had some who raised their voices on His behalf. Strangely enough, we would not think of them as being His friends, yet they spoke up for Him. Pilate's wife said, *"Have nothing to do with this Just Man, for I have suffered many things today in a dream because of Him"* (Mt. 27: 19). Pilate said, *"I find no fault in Him at all"* (Jn. 18:38). Herod decided that Jesus had not committed any capital crime (Lk. 23:15). One of the dying thieves said, *"This Man has done nothing wrong"* (Lk. 23:41). The centurion said, *"Certainly this was a righteous Man!"* (Lk. 23:47). And Judas, the doomed betrayer, wailed, *"I have sinned by betraying innocent blood"* (Mt. 27:4).

In the pit (Gen. 37:23–24)

In Joseph's case, they pulled off the offensive coat of many colors, threw him in a pit, and callously sat down for a meal, totally unconcerned. It wasn't a neat, antiseptic pit. The sun relentlessly beat down on it by day, and the cold engulfed it at night. There is no mention that the brothers gave him food and water. As the prophet Amos wrote, *"They were not grieved for the affliction of Joseph"* (Amos 6:6). They heard his pleas but were unmoved (Gen. 42:21).

In the Savior's case, the soldiers undressed Him and put a purple robe on Him in mockery of the kingship He claimed (Mt. 27:28). They crucified Him. Yes, they crucified Him. Then sitting down, they callously kept watch over Him as He hung on the cross in agony (Mt. 27:36). Once the show was over, the people went into the city, sat down, and ate the Passover meal, having just killed the Passover Lamb! Incredible!

The Lord Jesus likened His experience to being thrown into a pit, then being rescued from it. Speaking prophetically, the psalmist David pictured Him as saying:

I waited patiently for the Lord;
And He inclined to Me;
And heard My cry. He also brought Me up out of a horrible pit,
Out of the miry clay,
And set My feet upon a rock,
And established My steps (Ps. 40:1-2).

At this point in the narrative, there is a break in the typology. Joseph died only figuratively. The pit speaks of his death and burial. If he had actually died, he would not have been able to go to Egypt and become the savior of his people. Jesus, on the other hand, died literally. He tasted death to the full to become *"Savior of the world."*

The ugly fact is that when the Creator came to this planet to save His creatures, they turned on Him. It was not enough that they despised Him, harassed Him, pushed Him around, and insulted Him. They slapped and beat Him, covered His face with their filthy spittle, plowed His back into furrows with a scourge, and mocked Him with a crown of thorns. Then they exposed all the venom of sin that was in their hearts when they took their God to the place called Calvary and nailed Him to a cross.

> The ultimate crime! The supreme blasphemy! The vilest obscenity! The grossest stupidity! Sinners, perverted, defiled, and dead to God, actually nailed Him to the wood! He, the loveliest Man who ever walked the dust of earth, who healed their brokenhearted, dried their tears, and blessed their little children. He fed the hungry, and set their captives free. He brought the Word of heaven to their hearts and would open heaven to their souls. Who were these criminals? Our human race! (*J. Boyd Nicholson*).

Silent in his trials

The only recorded time in the sacred narrative when Joseph spoke out during this encounter with his brothers is when he pleaded for his life (Gen. 42:21). It is noteworthy that in the years to follow there is no suggestion that he ever criticized, blamed, or scathingly censured them. So it was with the Lord Jesus.

He was oppressed and He was afflicted,
Yet He opened not His mouth;
He was led as a lamb to the slaughter,
And as a sheep before its shearers is silent,
So He opened not His mouth (Isa. 53:7).

On trial before the high priest, He kept silent (Mt. 26:63). Accused by the chief priests and elders, He answered nothing (Mt. 27:12). Pilate marveled that Jesus did not answer him one word (Mt. 27:14). Herod *"questioned Him with many words, but He answered him nothing"* (Lk. 23:9). *"When He was reviled,* [He] *did not revile in return"* (1 Pet. 2:23). Only when the high priest put Him under oath and asked, *"...tell us if You are the Christ, the Son of God"* (Mt. 26:63) did Jesus reply:[4]

It is as you said. Nevertheless, I say to you, hereafter you will see the Son of Man sitting at the right hand of the Power, and coming on the clouds of heaven (Mt. 26:64).

Lord Jesus, I worship You for such self-control. It is utterly foreign to this world—and to me by nature.

Forsaken (Gen. 37:28)

Callous, heartless brothers, they turned their backs on Joseph. The fact that they were blood relatives did not concern them now. They were venting their spleen on him, getting even for imagined wrongs.

A better Man than Joseph endured similar treatment.

Speaking of Christ's disciples at Calvary, Mark marveled, *"They all forsook Him, and fled"* (Mk. 14:50). Jesus, however, endured a forsaking that Joseph never had to experience. It was during the three hours of darkness when His God forsook Him as He paid the penalty of our sins. It was when He cried, *"My God, My God, why have You forsaken Me?"* (Mt. 27:46).

> Yea, once, Immanuel's orphaned cry
> His universe hath shaken—
> It went up single, echoless,
> *"My God, I am forsaken."*
> —*Elizabeth Barrett Browning*

God forsook the Lord Jesus so that we might never be forsaken. Now we hear the loving Savior assure us, *"I will never leave you, nor forsake you"* (Heb. 13:5).

Betrayed

Although Joseph was their brother, they betrayed that intimate, natural relationship. He trusted them; they betrayed that confidence. He had done nothing wrong; they betrayed that innocence. Here again the experience of Jesus is mirrored. He was betrayed by one of His disciples. His own familiar friend, in whom He trusted, lifted up his heel against Him (Ps. 41:9). Judas was the one of whom David spoke prophetically in Psalm 55:

> *For it is not an enemy who reproaches me;*
> *Then I could bear it.*
> *Nor is it one who hates me who has exalted himself against me;*

Then I could hide from him.

But it was you, a man my equal,

My companion and my acquaintance.

We took sweet counsel together,

And walked to the house of God in the throng...

He has put forth his hands against those who were at peace with him;

He has broken his covenant.

The words of his mouth were smoother than butter,

But war was in his heart;

His words were softer than oil,

Yet they were drawn swords (vv. 12-14, 20-21).

Judas is a solemn example of how close a person can be to Christ and still be lost. He lived with the Lord, heard His incomparable teaching, and saw His unparalleled miracles. But he was a terrible imposter, the one who betrayed his God with a kiss.

Sold for silver (Gen. 37:28)

Some correspondences or similarities are inescapable. Joseph's brothers sold him to traveling Midianite traders for twenty pieces of silver, two-thirds the price of an average adult slave. Why kill him when you can profit financially by selling him?

The price of the Savior was thirty pieces of silver, the redemption price of a slave who had been gored by an ox (Ex. 21:32). Awful bargain! Judas was the one who arranged the sale. Judah and Judas are different forms of the same name. It means *praise*, which here seems terribly out of place.

THIRTY PIECES OF SILVER

Thirty pieces of silver
For the Lord of life they gave;
Thirty pieces of silver—
Only the price of a slave!
But it was the priestly value
Of the Holy One of God;
They weighed it out in the temple,
The price of the Savior's blood.

Thirty pieces of silver
Laid in Iscariot's hand;
Thirty pieces of silver
And the aid of an armed band,
Like a lamb that is led to the slaughter
Brought the humbled Son of God
At midnight from the garden,
Where His sweat had been like blood.

Thirty pieces of silver
Burn on the traitor's brain;
Thirty pieces of silver!
O it is hellish gain!
"I have sinned and betrayed the guiltless!"
He cried, with a fevered breath;
And he cast them down in the temple,
And rushed to a madman's death.

Thirty pieces of silver
Lay in the House of God;

JOSEPH'S EARLY LIFE

Thirty pieces of silver
But O 'twas the price of blood!
And so for a place to bury
The strangers in they gave
The price of their own Messiah,
Who lay in a borrowed grave.

It may not be for silver,
It may not be for gold,
But still by tens of thousands
Is this precious Savior sold.
Sold for a godless friendship,
Sold for a selfish aim,
Sold for a fleeting trifle,
Sold for an empty name,
Sold in the mart of Science,
Sold in the seat of power,
Sold at the shrine of Fortune,
Sold in pleasure's bower,
Sold where the awful bargain
None but God's eye can see!
Ponder, my soul, the question:
Shall He be sold by thee?
Sold, O God, what a moment!
Stifled is conscience' voice!
Sold! And a weeping angel
Records the fatal choice!
Sold! But the price of the Savior
To a living coal shall turn,
With the pangs of remorse forever
Deep in the soul to burn.   *—Wm. Blane*

By the end of chapter 36, the brothers probably thought that their treachery to Joseph was a well-guarded secret. They had a good alibi and there was no body, no physical evidence against them. They carried on from day to day, smugly assured that the chapter titled, Joseph, was closed.

Risen (Gen. 37:28)

God had not forgotten Joseph. By a marvelous set of designed circumstances, He controlled the minds of some foreign traders, their route, and speed so that they reached young Joseph at the proper time. F. B. Meyer sees in this a comforting truth for all God's people:

> It was not chance, but providence that brought these Midianites to the pit at that hour. They had, of course, fixed their time of departure from their native land, the speed at which their camels were to travel, and the amount of time which they would spend at the fairs and markets en route, quite irrespectively of all other considerations but their own profit and convenience; yet quite unconsciously they were moving according to a divine timetable. Everything in life is directed, superintended and controlled by a divine forethought. Let us live in constant recognition of this![5]

The empty pit (Gen. 37:29)

Later, when Reuben returned to the pit, he saw that it was empty. By now his brother was bumping along in a wagon to Egypt. God was preparing the stage for one of the great dramas of Bible history.

Figuratively, Joseph had risen from the dead. I don't have to tell you what this foreshadows. The application to our living Savior is in Luke 24:1-8:

Now on the first day of the week, very early in the morning, they, and certain other women with them, came to the tomb bringing the spices which they had prepared. But they found the stone rolled away from the tomb. Then they went in and did not find the body of the Lord Jesus. And it happened, as they were greatly perplexed about this, that behold, two men stood by them in shining garments. Then, as they were afraid and bowed their faces to the earth, they said to them, "Why do you seek the living among the dead? He is not here, but is risen! Remember how He spoke to you when He was still in Galilee, saying, 'The Son of Man must be delivered into the hands of sinful men, and be crucified, and the third day rise again.'" And they remembered His words.

Joseph was saved from dying. Christ was saved out of death. His grave is vacant now. God would not leave His soul in Hades [that is, disembodied], nor would He allow His Holy One [that is, His body] to see corruption (Acts 2:27).

Joseph's *"grave,"* *i.e.*, the pit, was only borrowed. He would not need it very long. So it was with the garden tomb. It was a loan from Joseph of Arimathea. Jesus would only need it for three days and three nights.

> They borrowed a room on His way to the tomb,
> The Passover lamb to eat;
> They borrowed a cave[6] to give Him a grave,
> They borrowed a winding sheet;
> But the crown that He wore
> And the cross that He bore
> Were His own—the cross was His own.
>
> —*Author unknown*

29

It seems strange to think of a borrowed tomb. Usually a tomb is for all time. There are no second-hand graves. Jesus did not need the gift of a grave. A borrowed one would do.

The witness of the blood (Gen. 37:31-33)

The brothers took Joseph's coat, dipped it in the blood of a young goat, and presented it to their father. It was a heartless ploy to make the old man think that Joseph had been eaten by a wild animal and that the sons were totally innocent.

The difference here is one of contrast, not comparison. Christ's blood has also been presented to the Father, but figuratively. He entered heaven, *"not with the blood of goats and calves, but with His blood He entered the Most Holy Place once for all, having obtained eternal redemption"* (Heb. 9:12). His blood was shed on Calvary but *the value of that blood* is what He took into the Most Holy Place.

> Peace with God, the blood in heaven
> Speaks of pardon now to me;
> Peace with God! The Lord is risen!
> Righteousness now counts me free.
>
> —A. P. Cecil

Lame explanations (Gen. 37:32-33)

The brothers told their father that a wild animal must have destroyed Joseph. True, there was blood on the coat, but how did the animal devour him without shredding his garment? The explanation didn't make sense. The one-time trickster Jacob must have been canny enough to see that it was lame, but what could he do?

The oldest attempt to deny the resurrection of Christ is in Matthew 28:13, 15. The chief priests bribed the Roman soldiers to say that the disciples stole the body while they were sleeping. If that was true, why did the religious leaders have to bribe the soldiers to tell the truth? And why were the soldiers sleeping when they should have been on duty? To sleep on watch was a capital offense.

A second attempt to discredit the resurrection is the "swoon theory." It says that Jesus didn't actually die. He merely lost consciousness and then the coolness of the tomb revived Him. But the soldiers knew He was dead and that is why they didn't break His legs. Even if He had only swooned, how did He move the huge stone that sealed the tomb and get past the soldiers? By then He was not a Man in full strength, and His lifeblood had been drained away. How could a bloodless corpse leave the tomb?

Then there is the theory that the women went to the wrong tomb. This overlooks the fact that it was not one of many tombs in a cemetery, but an isolated tomb in a private garden. Were the soldiers and the angels and the other disciples also at the wrong tomb? And if it was the wrong tomb, why didn't the Jewish leaders expose it by going to the right one?

Solomon said that *"the legs of the lame are not equal"* (Prov. 26:7), which is true of all skeptical attacks on the resurrection. Such attacks are lame because the theories do not conform to the facts. Would the disciples be willing to die for such lame explanations as these?

Take a moment here to marvel at the many ways in which Joseph's life foreshadowed the life of the Lord Jesus more than 1700 years later. Can you imagine anyone today who could write such a record of a Person who will live in AD 3700? The conclusion is inevitable. The story of Joseph reveals the finger of God.

Chapter Two

INTERLUDE

The story of Joseph is interrupted in chapter 38. Here we have the sordid account of Judah's sin with Tamar and its painful results. Coming between the rejection of Joseph and his eventual reconciliation with his brothers, it describes the moral condition of the nation of Israel since its rejection of the Messiah. It pictures God's ancient people during the present time when they are cast away, when He calls Israel *Lo-ammi*—not My people (Hos. 1:9).

Judah's first sin was in marrying a Gentile, contrary to the law of God. Three sons were born, the oldest of which married a Hebrew woman named Tamar. When he died, she married the second son, but he refused to perpetuate the family name and inheritance. Judah promised her the third son when he became of age. But when he failed to keep his promise, she disguised herself as a harlot and seduced him. As payment he promised to send her a young goat. Until then he gave her his signet, cord, and staff as a pledge.

When he tried to send the goat to her and repossess the pledge, she could not be found. Later, news came to him that his daughter-in-law had played the harlot. He impulsively cursed her to die, but she forestalled that by producing his pledge and exposing him as the father. She bore two sons, Perez and Zerah. What a can of worms! Yet look carefully at the genealogy of our Lord in Matthew 1, and you will find the name Perez (v. 3). Only God is able to bring good out of such moral chaos.

Chapter Three

JOSEPH'S LIFE IN EGYPT

Returning now to Joseph, we see him carried to Egypt by the Midianite caravan. That was providential. The future was all unknown to him, but God lies behind the scenes, moving the checkers on the board of history. All His trains run on schedule.

Asylum in Egypt (Gen. 39:1).

God, who foresees the future, had to get Joseph to Egypt to work out His purposes in preserving His people. Joseph found safety there.

The Son of Man also found asylum in Egypt when Herod issued a decree to kill all male children in Bethlehem and its environs (Mt. 2:14-16). An angel of the Lord appeared to His stepfather in a dream, warning him to flee to Egypt. The family was there until the death of Herod, then returned to Canaan in fulfillment of the prophecy in Hosea 11:1, *"Out of Egypt I called My son."*

A bondslave (Gen. 39:1, 4)

Joseph became a servant of Potiphar, one of Pharaoh's officers. It would be correct to say that he was a bondslave, because Potiphar purchased him. He belonged to his master.

God's well-beloved Son came down from the splendor of heaven and became a bondslave. He who was in the form of God took the form of a servant (see Phil. 2). He did not come to be served, but to serve, and to give His life a ransom for many. He said, *"I am among you as One who serves"* (Lk. 22:27).

He is the perfect example of the Hebrew slave who could have obtained freedom but said, *"I love my master. I will not go out free"* (Ex. 21:5). It is He who girded Himself with a towel, the apron of a slave, and stooped to wash His disciples' feet. His greatest act of servanthood was His death for us all.

There is a difference between a hired servant and a bondslave. The hired servant works for pay. The bondslave works because he belongs to his master. In ancient Israel the bondslave was worth twice as much as the hired servant:

> *It shall not seem hard to you when you send him* [the bondslave] *away free from you; for he has been worth a double hired servant in serving you six years. Then the Lord your God will bless you in all that you do* (Deut. 15:18).

It is still true that those who serve the Lord out of love for Him are worth considerably more than those who do it for pay. It's a question of a person's motivation.

Delivered to the Gentiles (Gen. 39:1-4)

Joseph's own brothers had hated him without cause. In Egypt he was in the anomalous position of being employed by Gentiles. People who were despised by the Jews and treated as the scum of the earth found a place for him.

This mirrors the reception that the Lord Jesus received. It was Gentiles who were more receptive to Him than the Jews. At His birth, Gentile wise men came to Him with gifts. Among His first converts were Gentiles: the woman at the well and some of her neighbors from Sychar. Twice He voiced surprise that it was Gentiles who put their faith in Him: when He healed the servant of a Roman centurion, He said to the officer, *"I say to you, I have not found such great faith, not even in Israel"* (Lk. 7:9). When He met a Canaanite woman in the region of Tyre and Sidon, and delivered her demon-possessed daughter, He said, *"O woman, great is your faith"* (Mt. 15:28). After He healed ten lepers, only one of them returned to thank Him, and that one was a Gentile. Even at the cross a Roman officer said, *"Truly this was the Son of God"* (Mt. 27:54).

Power and prominence (Gen. 39:2-4)

Tyndale's 1534 translation of verse 2 reads, "The Lord was with Joseph and he was a luckie fellow." Luck, however, played no role in Joseph's life nor does it in the lives of any of God's people. Divine wisdom, love, and power planned his life. The New King James Version of verse 2 reads: *"The Lord was with Joseph, and he was a suc-*

37

cessful man." The Lord made all he did to prosper. His master put him in charge of everything in his house. Even when Joseph was imprisoned unjustly, it is repeated that the Lord was with him. The warden put him in charge of the other inmates (Gen. 39:21-23). After his release, he rose to be second in command to the reigning monarch (Gen. 41:40). In later years he would rise to greater exaltation. Through all his life, he could say in the words of Andrew Murray, "I am here by God's appointment, in His keeping, under His training, for His time."

Just as Pharaoh realized that the Spirit of God was in Joseph (Gen. 41:38), so did Nicodemus see that God was with the Lord Jesus: *"No one can do these signs that You do unless God is with Him"* (Jn. 3:2).

Joseph was a clear prototype of the Christ of Calvary, whom God highly exalted. He has given Him the name that is above every name. He has committed all judgment to Him. And He has made Him to be Head over all things to the Church.

Blessings to the Gentiles (Gen. 39:5)
There is an interesting insight in Genesis 39:5:

> *So it was, from the time that he had made him overseer of his house and all that he had, that the Lord blessed the Egyptian's house for Joseph's sake; and the blessing of the Lord was on all that he had in the house and in the field.*

God blessed not only Joseph, He blessed those whom Joseph served. It seems that whenever he touched other lives, they were benefitted. He was a channel through which divine favor flowed to those whose path he crossed.

How true this is of our Savior. He came not only *"to confirm the promises made to the* [Hebrew] *fathers, but also that the Gentiles might glorify God for His mercy"* (Rom. 15:8–9). Through the fall of Israel, salvation has come to the Gentiles (Rom. 11:11). The Lord Jesus is the channel through which blessing flows from the Father (Rom. 5:1-2).

> Blessings abound where'er He reigns;
> The pris'ner leaps to loose his chains,
> The weary find eternal rest,
> And all the sons of want are blest.   —*Isaac Watts*

Handsome (Gen. 39:6)

Even if his brothers couldn't see it, Joseph was *"handsome in form and appearance."* An old preacher said, "Grace is a beautiful thing, and it loves a beautiful vessel in which to display itself." Grace found such a vessel in Joseph. He was handsome, both inwardly and outwardly.

We do not know the Lord's facial appearance. There is no authentic picture of Him. I personally believe He is handsome. But this may seem to be contradicted by Isaiah 53:2b:

> *He has no form or comeliness; and when we see Him, there is no beauty that we should desire Him.*

This, however, is how the nation of Israel regarded Him when He, the Messiah, came to earth. They could see no beauty in Him, but that doesn't mean it wasn't there. It's just that they weren't in the proper condition to recognize His beauty, either physically or spiritually. To us He will always be *"the fairest of the sons of men"* (Ps. 45:2).

> Fairest of all the earth-born race,
> Perfect in comeliness Thou art;
> Replenished are Thy lips with grace
> And full of love Thy tender heart.
> Forever blest, we bow the knee
> And own all fullness dwells in Thee.
>
> —*Author unknown*

Strong temptation (Gen. 39:7-12a)

Potiphar's wife cast lustful glances at Joseph and for days tried to seduce him to sin with her. Finally she grabbed hold of his coat. Incidentally, this is the second mention of a garment in the life of Joseph, and both of them caused him trouble, through no fault of his own. Both were used to deceive. There are two more mentions of garments in his career—prison garments and robes of glory and honor.

Joseph's divine Counterpart, the Son of Man, was also faced with strong temptation (Mt. 4:1-11). After Jesus had fasted 40 days and nights, the devil appeared to Him with three temptations:

• The lust of the eyes: worship me and get the kingdoms of the world.
• The lust of the flesh: command these stones to become bread.

• The pride of life: tempt God by jumping from the temple pinnacle.

In these three ways the Savior was tempted from without. But unlike Joseph and us, He could not be tempted from within. There was nothing in Him to respond to evil solicitation. When it says in Hebrews 4:15 that "[He] *was in all points tempted as we are,*" we must remember that they were outward temptations only.

People argue that although Christ didn't sin, He could have sinned. They say it wasn't a real test if He could not sin. But that is a human reasoning. Think of the following: Jesus is God; can God sin? If He could have sinned as a Man here on earth, why can't He sin as a Man in heaven? If He could sin, does that mean that He could commit *any* sin—murder, fornication, or robbery? Even the thought is blasphemous.

A man of purity and integrity (Gen. 39:12b)

Joseph had strong reasons for resisting his master's wife: his master trusted him (v. 8); he had an exalted position (v. 9a) and privilege obligates; the woman was married to his master (v.9b); it would have been sin against God (v. 9). Joseph was always faithful to his God.

Our Lord also had strong reasons for resisting temptation. His faithfulness to God the Father required it. To yield would have disqualified Him from being our Savior and would have thwarted the purpose of His incarnation. He must fulfill the Scriptures concerning His sinless humanity.

Yes, spotless, undefiled, and pure,
The great Redeemer stood,
While Satan's fiery darts He bore,
And did resist to blood.

—*Isaac Watts*

Joseph's response to temptation was to leave his garment in the woman's hand and to flee. As one quaint preacher put it, "Sometimes it isn't fight the good fight; it is flee the good flight."

William Congreve observed that hell has no fury like a woman scorned. Was he right? Read on.

Suffering for righteousness' sake (Gen. 39:13-20)

The woman then falsely accused Joseph to her husband, using the abandoned coat as circumstantial evidence. Without any inquiry, Potiphar had him thrown into a filthy, foul dungeon. It was a classic miscarriage of justice, and a clear example of suffering for righteousness. Joseph had done no wrong. As he said, *"I have done nothing here that they should put me into the dungeon"* (Gen. 40:15).

This was a clear case of suffering for doing good. Centuries later, the apostle Peter speaks of it in his first letter:

> *For this is commendable, if because of conscience toward God one endures grief, suffering wrongfully. For what credit is it if, when you are beaten for your faults, you take it patiently? But when you do good and suffer for it, if you take it patiently, this is commendable before God* (1 Pet. 2:19-20).

No one ever suffered more for righteousness than our beloved Lord. There was never a more egregious miscarriage of justice than when God Incarnate was betrayed, falsely accused, found to be innocent, then beaten and crucified as a felon. As Peter wrote,

> *He committed no sin, nor was deceit found in His mouth, who, when He was reviled, did not revile in return; when He suffered, He did not threaten, but committed Himself to Him who judges righteously; who Himself bore our sins in His own body on the tree, that we, having died to sins, might live for righteousness—by whose stripes you were healed* (1 Pet. 2:22-24).

Suffering at the hands of the Gentiles (Gen. 39:20)

The Egyptian judicial system found him guilty, although if Potiphar was really convinced of his guilt, he probably would have had him executed.

Joseph in the pit in Canaan typifies the Savior's crucifixion at the hands of His Jewish brethren (Acts 2:23, 36). Joseph in the prison in Egypt prefigures our Lord's suffering at the hand of the Gentiles:

> *For truly against Your holy Servant Jesus, whom You anointed, both Herod and Pontius Pilate, with the Gentiles were gathered together"* (Acts 4:27).

But, as we have seen, these rulers were not personally convinced of His guilt. Had they fully realized what they were doing, they would not have crucified the Lord of glory (1 Cor. 2:8).

Jesus was never in prison. When Isaiah wrote, *"He was taken from prison and judgment..."* (Isa. 53:8), it does

43

not mean that He was taken out of prison. Rather He was hurried away from any contact with prison and with justice, and thus denied the extra time that incarceration would have provided. His enemies made it impossible for Him to have a fair trial.

Numbered with transgressors (Gen. 40:1-3)

In prison with Joseph were the king's butler and baker, there for some unnamed offenses. Here, too, he makes us think of Christ who was crucified between two criminals. Many years later when Mark described Calvary (15:28), he remembered Isaiah 53:12 and wrote, *"And He was numbered with the transgressors."* But Christ did not die for any personal misdeeds. He had none.

Two guilty prisoners (Gen. 40:1)

The butler and baker had offended the king, and he was angry. Neither one of them protested his innocence. Only Joseph could say, *"I have done nothing here that they should put me into the dungeon"* (Gen. 40:15).

In the case of the transgressors who were crucified with our innocent Lord, Matthew and Mark say they were robbers (Mt. 27:38; Mk. 15:27-28). Luke describes them as criminals (Lk. 23:32-33, 39). One of them admitted they were receiving the just rewards of their deeds. That man was saved; the other perished.

An interpreter (Gen. 40:9-19)

The butler and baker had dreams about Pharaoh and their service for him, but they needed someone to interpret the dreams. How remarkable that Joseph was the right man in the right place at the right time. His power to interpret came from God, however, and not from himself (Gen. 40:8). We must not misunderstand him when he said, *"Do not interpretations belong to God? Tell them* [the dreams] *to me, please."*

At first this might sound as if he was claiming to be God. What he meant was: "God is the One who interprets dreams. If you tell me what you dreamt, God will reveal the meaning to me and I will tell you."

When they obeyed, Joseph assured the butler that the king would lift his head in restoration to his former position. He would also lift up the baker's head, but for him it would be execution rather than exaltation. To borrow Paul's words, Joseph was *"to the one the aroma of death to death, and to the other the aroma of life to life"* (2 Cor. 2:16). So believers are *"to God the fragrance of Christ among those who are being saved and among those who are perishing"* (2:15). Stop and ask yourself, Am I being saved or am I perishing?

Just as Joseph foretold their future, so the Lord Jesus reveals what lies ahead. *"The testimony of Jesus is the spirit of prophecy"* (Rev. 1:10). He makes clear to everyone where he or she will spend eternity. Heaven for those who believe in Him. Hell for those who don't.

Our Lord Jesus was an interpreter of God the Father. John made this clear when he wrote in his Gospel:

No one has seen God at any time. The only begotten Son, who is in the bosom of the Father, He has declared Him (1:18).

45

Jesus spoke the message that the Father wanted Him to reveal (Jn. 12:49-50). He told the disciples what He had heard from His Father (Jn. 15:15). It was a matter of conveying the very words of the Father. He performed the works ordained by the Father (Jn. 14:10). When we have seen Him, we have seen the Father (Jn. 14:9). Just as Joseph gave the entire honor to God, so did the Lord Jesus (Jn. 17:4).

Joseph was in prison because of the sins of others. The woman's lust and lies, and her husband's gullibility in believing her (or at least not standing up to her if he knew she was lying) put Joseph behind bars. Potiphar accepted the testimony of one person. He should have known that competent testimony is found in the words of two or three witnesses (Mt. 18:16).

"Remember me" (Gen. 40:14)

After predicting the restoration of the chief butler, Joseph made a simple request: *"But remember me when it is well with you"* (Gen. 40:14). It was not asking too much, considering what Joseph had done for him.

It is more than coincidence that in this passage where we have the words, *"Remember me,"* we have an indirect reference to bread and wine. The baker was the one who made the bread for the palace residents. The butler was the king's wine taster.

This association of bread and wine with the words *"Remember me"* point inescapably to the Lord's Supper. On the night of His betrayal, our Savior instituted what some have called the Communion Service. He used bread as a symbol of His body given in death for us. The wine signifies the New Covenant which was ratified by His blood shed on the cross. He said, *"Do this in remembrance of Me"* (Lk. 22:19). The apostle Paul gives the added instruction, *"For as often as you eat this bread and drink this cup, you proclaim the Lord's death until He comes."* It is not asking too much, is it, considering all He has done for us? And remembering His promise, *"You will not be forgotten by Me"* (Isa. 44:21).

As to the frequency of the service, the Lord simply said, *"As often as..."* The apostles and early disciples adopted the policy of doing it every Lord's Day, or the first day of the week (Acts 20:7). If we follow their example, we will remember Him in this way every Sunday.

But that is not the only time we will remember Him. Anytime Calvary comes into our minds, we remember Him. The Lord's Supper, however, is a special remembrance, an act of obedience to the dying request of the Redeemer. As to the duration of this ordinance, it is *"till He comes."*

When Paul says, *"We proclaim His death,"* he implies that unbelievers may be present, though not participating.

The sad ending of the episode involving Joseph and the butler is that the butler did not remember Joseph. We can escape a similarly sad memory lapse by faithfully remembering our Lord in the Breaking of Bread. It is our response of love to the One who died for us.

Fetters of iron

In Psalm 105:18, we have a detail concerning Joseph's

JOSEPH MAKES ME THINK OF JESUS

imprisonment that we would not otherwise know: *"They hurt his feet with fetters, he was laid in irons."* This shows that it was not simple confinement and isolation. The prison was not like our Federal Prisons today where even the inmates call them Club Fed. In Joseph's time a prison meant harsh punishment and cruel fetters.

Little did Joseph know he was having fellowship with the sufferings of the coming Messiah, who said prophetically, *"They pierced My hands and My feet"* (Ps. 22:16).

> His hands were pierced, the hands that made
> The mountain range and everglade;
> That washed the stains of sin away,
> And changed earth's darkness into day.
>
> His feet were pierced, the feet that trod
> The farthest shining star of God:
> And left their imprint deep and clear
> On ev'ry winding pathway here.
>
> His heart was pierced, the heart that burned
> To comfort ev'ry heart that yearned;
> And from it came a cleansing flood,
> The river of redeeming blood.
>
> His hands and feet and heart, all three
> Were pierced for me on Calvary,
> And here and now to Him I bring
> My heart, my feet, an offering. —*Author unknown*

Tested by the Word (Ps. 105:19)

In the psalm we have just mentioned, it says, *"The*

word of the Lord tested him." How did the word test Joseph? First of all, the Lord had promised in the dreams of the sheaves and the solar system that he would be master over his brothers and parents. But he was subsequently thrown into a pit and then into prison, far removed from his family. The chances of his ever ruling over them seemed remote. He could have said, "If what God revealed to me in those dreams is true, what am I doing here?" It was a test of Joseph's faith in God's word. He stood firm.

This too, of course, has a parallel in the life of our Lord. God had promised that He would have universal dominion (Ps. 2:8; Zech. 9:10). Yet His life on earth up to the time of His burial gave little to confirm the promise. Yes, the word of God tested Him. A lesser person would have doubted. John the Baptist did. He sent two of his disciples to Jesus and asked. *"Are You the Coming One, or do we look for another?"* (Mt. 11:2-3). The Lord Jesus never wavered.

The Lord had the sorrow and testing of the contradiction of sinners continually, and had even to say that He had labored in vain, and spent His strength for naught and in vain; He had to see the cities wherein most of His mighty works had been done unmoved thereby. But *"At that time, Jesus answering said, I praise Thee, Father, Lord of the heaven and of the earth, that Thou hast hid these things from the wise and prudent, and hast revealed them to babes. Yea, Father for thus has it been well pleasing in Thy sight."* Under the testing there was nothing found in Him but perfect confidence in the way and sovereignty of His Father.[7]

Wonderful counselor (Gen. 41:1-36)

After three years in prison, the time arrived for Joseph's release. It came about as a result of a dream that the king had and which none of his wise men could interpret. At last the chief butler remembered Joseph and recommended him to the king. When called, Joseph predicted seven great harvest years, then seven years of scarcity. He also proposed a wise plan to ensure an ever-normal granary. By setting aside reserves in the plentiful years, Egypt would have food in the years of famine. Finally Joseph advised the king to appoint a man to administer the program. Pharaoh said, "You are the man."

Jesus is our wonderful Counselor (Isa. 9:6). He tells us how we can be sure we will never hunger and never thirst. He urges us to lay up treasures in heaven, not on earth. He provides us with all we need for life and godliness, for time and eternity.

A giant leap (Gen. 41:39-44)

Recognizing that the Spirit of God was in Joseph, Pharaoh released him from prison and appointed him to govern the kingdom. It was a giant leap—from the pit to the palace. Pharaoh said to Joseph:

> *Inasmuch as God has shown you all this, there is no one as discerning and wise as you.... "See, I have set you over all the land of Egypt."*
>
> *Then Pharaoh took his signet ring off his hand and put it on Joseph's hand; and he clothed him in garments of fine linen and put a gold chain around his neck. And he had him ride in the sec-*

ond chariot which he had; and they cried out before him, "Bow the knee!"

So he set him over all the land of Egypt. Pharaoh also said to Joseph, "I am Pharaoh, and without your consent no man may lift his hand or foot in all the land of Egypt" (Gen. 41:39, 41-44).

The signet ring was a symbol of authority, the fine linen of royal glory, and the gold chain of distinguished service and honor. Joseph was now *"the lord of all Egypt"* (Gen. 45:9).

This foreshadows the rise of God's Son from the cross to the throne. The Spirit of God prophesied through the psalmist David,

All the ends of the world shall remember and turn to the Lord, and all the families of the nations shall worship before You (Ps. 22:27).

Isaiah prophesied, *"The government shall be upon His shoulder"* (9:6). On the Day of Pentecost, Peter announced, *"God has made Him...both Lord and Christ"* (Acts 2:36) and later proclaimed, *"God has exalted [Him] to His right hand to be Prince and Savior"* (Acts 5:31). Paul insisted that God

...raised Him from the dead and seated Him at His right hand in the heavenly places, far above all principality and power and might, and dominion and every name that is named, not only in this age but also in that which is to come. And He put all things under His feet, and gave Him to be head over all things to the Church, which is His body, the fullness of Him who fills all in all (Eph. 1:20-23).

51

Quoting Isaiah 45:23, Paul also reminds us that the Lord has decreed, *"Every knee shall bow to Me, and every tongue shall confess to God"* (Rom. 14:11). The Apostle John quotes an angel as rejoicing, *"The kingdoms of this world have become the kingdoms of our Lord and of His Christ, and He shall reign forever and ever"* (Rev. 11:15). The Sufferer is now crowned with glory and honor (Heb. 2:9). "The Son of Man who was crucified is the King of glory now" (*J. G. Deck*). One day we will see Him honored by the whole creation. What a day of rejoicing that will be!

> All of this happened because one day, for the sake of God, Joseph resisted a temptation to one act of sin. If he had yielded, we should probably never have heard of him again; he would have been slain by the siren who has slain so many more strong men. Let us seek first the kingdom of God and His righteousness. He will turn again and have mercy upon us, and will exalt us to inherit the earth.[8]

"Go to Joseph" (Gen. 41:40)

The king entrusted Joseph with the keys to all the treasure houses of Egypt. If anyone needed bread, the word was, *"Go to Joseph; whatever he says to you, do"* (Gen. 41:55).

The Lord Jesus is our Joseph. He is the living bread which came down from heaven (Jn. 6:51). All the treasures of wisdom and knowledge are hidden in Him (Col. 2:3). *"The Father has given all things into His hands"* (Jn. 3:35). It is in Him that we are blessed with every spiritual blessing in the heavenlies (Eph. 1:3).

A fullness resides in Jesus our Head,
A fullness abides to answer all need:
The Father's good pleasure has laid up a store,
A plentiful treasure, to give to the poor.

—Fawcett

The king's words find an echo in Mary's advice at the wedding in Cana of Galilee: *"Whatever He says to you, do it"* (Jn. 2:5).

Bow the knee (Gen. 41:43).

As Joseph rode along in the second chariot, Pharaoh's men ordered the people to bow the knee to him. Everyone must bow to him. Potiphar's wife must bow to him. What a humiliating turning of the tables! Potiphar must bow to him, the same one who had imprisoned him. The Egyptians, who considered the Hebrews an abomination, must bow to him. All must bow to the once despised and rejected one.

"Bow the knee!" the herald cried, as Joseph, arrayed in his robes of state and official regalia, was driven in the royal chariot through the land of Egypt. And woe to that man or woman who refused to bow to the former Hebrew slave. Potiphar's wife would have to bow with the rest before that one whom she had so wickedly sought to ruin. And those proud knees will bow to Jesus Christ, the Son of God, that now "take Him a creature to be," and do their best to make the world believe that He is not what He said He was, though the Holy Spirit proclaims Him *"God manifest in the flesh!"* O, how will it fare in that day with these lying traducers of His holy Person, these deniers of His deity, these shameless

'higher critics' who pretend to know more than He, when they come to bow themselves before Him? How will they cringe before His presence when He sits upon His judgment throne, and it is made manifest what hard speeches they have ungodly spoken against Him?[9]

The Sovereign has made a royal command:

...that at the name of Jesus every knee should bow, of those in heaven, and of those on earth, and of those under the earth, and that every tongue should confess that Jesus Christ is Lord, to the glory of God the Father (Phil. 2:10-11).

It happens either now or at the Judgment of the Great White Throne. It happens either willingly now or it will happen by compulsion then.

> At the name of Jesus ev'ry knee shall bow,
> Ev'ry tongue confess Him King of glory now;
> 'Tis the Father's pleasure we should call Him Lord,
> Who from the beginning was the mighty Word.
> —*Caroline M. Noel*

The Spirit of God (Gen. 41:38)

When Joseph spelled out his program to prepare for the seven years of famine, Pharaoh was impressed. Turning to his assistants, he said, *"Can we find a man such as this in whom is the Spirit of God?"* (Gen. 41:38). But how would this heathen monarch know about the Spirit of God? Perhaps this is a case where the pagan ruler spoke beyond his own knowledge of biblical matters, but what he said was true. Joseph's wisdom and expertise showed that God was with him, counseling and empowering him.

How much truer this is of the Lord Jesus. Although eternally one with the Father and the Spirit, yet the Holy Spirit came upon Him at His baptism, preparing Him for the ministry that lay ahead (Mt. 3:16, 17). God gave Him the Spirit without measure (Jn. 3:34).

At the beginning of His public ministry He quoted those beautiful verses from Isaiah 61:1-3 and applied them to Himself:

The Spirit of the Lord God is upon Me, because the Lord has anointed Me to preach good tidings to the poor; He has sent Me to heal the brokenhearted, to proclaim liberty to the captives, and the opening of the prison to those who are bound; to proclaim the acceptable year of the Lord, and the day of vengeance of our God; to comfort all who mourn, to console those who mourn in Zion, to give them beauty for ashes, the oil of joy for mourning, the garment of praise for the spirit of heaviness, that they may be called trees of righteousness, the planting of the Lord, that He may be glorified.

The Name above every name

Is it proper to refer to Him as Jesus or should we always give Him his full title—Lord Jesus Christ? Perhaps we turn away from using the single name *"Jesus"* because we hear other believers saying the name in a way that seems to us to be repetitive, frivolous, and irreverent. But we must not judge. Those Christians may love and worship Him with true, heartfelt devotion.

Actually there is scriptural support for referring to Him simply as Jesus. To give a few examples: Eph. 4:21;

1 Thess. 1:10; 4:14; Heb. 6:20; 7:22; 10:19; 12:2, 24; 13:12; Rev. 14:12; 17:6; 19:10; 20:4.

Jesus is the name above every name. It is the name that commands universal obeisance and confession. Must we abandon it because of how others use it?

We do not hesitate to use the name in our hymns. A surprising number of sacred songs address our Lord as Jesus, and no one feels that it is improper.

What is the conclusion? While it is fitting to refer to our Savior by His full title, we should not hesitate to call Him Jesus, as long as we do so reverently. To quote a children's chorus, "When we call Him Jesus, we call Him by His name."

A new name (Gen. 41:45)

The new name which Pharaoh gave Joseph was Zaphnath-Paaneah. There is uncertainty as to the meaning of the name. Some say it means "revealer of secrets." Others suggest "sustainer of life." Josephus understood it to mean "the savior of the world." All are appropriate. They fit Joseph well.

The ultimate and unique Savior of the world has the name that is above every name, the name of Jesus. There is no mistaking the meaning of that name. It is "Jehovah is Savior." By His work at Calvary, He acquired it as a new name. He could never have had it if He had remained in heaven.

A Gentile bride (Gen. 41:45)

Not least of the honors heaped upon Joseph was the

gift of a Gentile bride, Asenath. She was the daughter of Poti-pherah, a heathen priest as well as an officer of Pharaoh. It was not usual for a Jewish man to marry a Gentile, but in this case God ordained it. It is significant that Joseph received his bride while his brothers were set aside, as far as the record is concerned.

Like Joseph, the Lord Jesus came to His own but His own would not receive Him. As mentioned previously, He found more faith in some of the Gentiles than He did in Jews. So it is that the Church, His bride, is composed mostly of Gentiles who have come to saving faith in Him. This does not mean that God is through with Israel. At the present time, however, Israel is set aside and He is calling out of the nations (Gentiles) a people for His name. No bride was ever bought at such an exorbitant price as the Church.

> Thy Father, in His gracious love,
> Did spare Thee from His side;
> And Thou didst stoop to bear above,
> At such a cost Thy bride.
> —*Mary Bowley Peters*

From suffering to glory (Gen. 41:43)

When we see Joseph as the lord of all Egypt, it is easy to forget all the suffering he endured—first from his own brothers, then from malicious, ungrateful people in Egypt.

Isn't that what happened in the case of the Lord Jesus? Peter tells how the Old Testament prophets indicated beforehand *"the sufferings of Christ and the glories that should follow"* (1 Pet. 1:11). The cross must precede the glory. First must come the altar of sacrifice, then the throne.

Tireless travels (Gen. 41:45)

Davis comments, "One cannot help but be impressed by Joseph's ingenious administration, to say nothing of the boundless energy with which he traveled throughout the land while preparing for the famine."[10]

As a result of his skillful leadership under the blessing of God, *"the ground brought forth abundantly"* (41:47). He *"gathered very much grain, as the sand of the sea, until he stopped counting, for it was without number"* (41:49).

Joseph's travels picture the young Nazarene's three years' journeys in Galilee, Perea, and Judea, working the works of Him who sent Him while it was day. Ever since sin entered, His father had been working and so must He (Jn. 5:17). Mark's Gospel especially presents Him as the tireless Servant, filling every day with works of faith and love.

And the Lord Jesus is the Great Gatherer, calling an innumerable multitude out of every tribe, tongue, people, and nation and redeeming them by His precious blood.

Forget and be fruitful (Gen. 41:51-52)

Joseph had two sons, Manasseh and Ephraim. Manasseh means "forgetting." God made Joseph forget his troubles, sorrows, and the wrongs against him.

Ephraim means "fruitfulness." God caused Joseph to be fruitful. Instead of holding grudges and becoming hard, cold, bitter, and cynical, he prospered and became productive for God. The lesson here is that we must forget wrongs against us if we want to be fruitful for God.

No one was ever more forgiving and forgetting than the Redeemer. Even in the hour of His passion, He cried, *"Father, forgive them for they do not know what they are doing."* No one was ever more forgiving and fruitful than He. He was fruitful in His offspring. In Isaiah 8:18, we hear Him say, *"Here am I and the children whom God has given Me."* He brings many sons to glory (Heb. 2:10). Those who crucified Him thought He would have no posterity since He was dying as a single Man, but Isaiah triumphantly announces, *"He shall see His seed, He shall prolong His days, and the pleasure of the Lord shall prosper in His hand"* (53:10b).

Famine (Gen. 41:54)

God did not send the famine. No evil comes from Him. But He permitted it to come and controlled its timing perfectly. It arrived just as Joseph had predicted. It struck worldwide, but Joseph's preparation sufficed, for in that country of the Nile, there was bread and to spare.

Likewise every prophecy of the Lord Jesus comes to pass. Not one word of His ever falls to the ground. He has predicted seven years of tribulation on the world prior to His advent in glory. They will surely come to pass, but there is safety through faith in Him. Just as it was after Joseph received a bride that the famine came, so it will be after Jesus receives His bride at the Rapture that the Tribulation will begin. With that in mind, notice how the periods of Joseph's life appear to suggest the following flow of history and prophecy:

- the seven years of plenty: the present Church age.
- Joseph receives a Gentile bride: the pre-Tribulation Rapture of the church.
- the seven years of famine: the seven-year Tribulation.
- Joseph makes himself known to his brothers: Christ's Second Advent, *i.e.*, His pre-millennial coming to reign when Israel will be regathered to the land.
- His care for his brothers in Goshen: the Millennium when the Messiah lovingly cares for His own.

The famine was a tool in God's hand to empty the pantry in Jacob's home, to set in motion the chariot wheels to take his sons from Canaan to Egypt, and eventually to bring the brothers and all of Jacob's family face to face with Joseph. It was only the first in a series of trials and tribulations cleverly designed to cause Jacob's ten sons to confess their guilt and restore fellowship with their estranged brother.

Age thirty (Gen. 41:46)

Was it a coincidence that Joseph was thirty years old when he stood before Pharaoh and began his service for the realm? Or was it the Spirit of God, who wrote the book of Genesis, superintending the life of Joseph so that he would be an undeniable type of the Lord Jesus? Luke tells us that *"Jesus Himself began His ministry at about thirty years of age"* (Lk. 3:23). Age thirty has been a crisis time in the lives of many of God's people. It is a time when they ask, "What am I doing with my life? Am I spinning my wheels or am I making my life count for God?" They have tasted what the world has to offer and now they want something better.

Plenty for all (Gen. 41:57)

The narrative now moves from the years of plenty to the time of famine. The seven years of plenty picture *"the acceptable year of the Lord"* while the second seven point to *"the day of vengeance of our God."* When Jesus spoke in the synagogue in Nazareth, He announced the acceptable year of the Lord. This is the age in which we now live, introduced by His first advent.

Picture hordes of people coming from famine-stricken lands to buy grain in Egypt. Not one of them was refused.

Now hear the Lord Jesus announce, *"I am the bread of life. He who comes to Me shall never hunger, and he who believes in Me shall never thirst"* (Jn. 6:35). After all the centuries, the invitation still rings out, *"Come, buy and eat without money and without price"* (Isa. 55:1). Have you responded by acknowledging your spiritual famine and by feeding on Christ, the living Bread?

Chapter Four

THE FIRST TRIP OF JOSEPH'S BROTHERS TO EGYPT

There was no mention of Jacob and the brothers in chapters 39-41. They were cast aside, but not forever, as we shall see. Now the scene changes from Egypt to Canaan. In a time of worldwide famine, Joseph's father heard that there was plenty of food in Egypt. So he decided to send all his sons except Benjamin to buy grain. They had little choice—it was either buy or die.

They arrived in Egypt and stood before the governor, little knowing he was their brother. He spoke roughly to them at first and accused them of being spies. As if shooting an arrow at random, he asked them if their father was still alive and if they had another brother (43:7). Of all the questions he could have asked, none would have been more unsettling!

The brothers picture the people of Israel at the present

time. They are cast aside, but not finally. Judicial blindness has come upon them because of their refusal to accept the Messiah. Paul says,

> ...*their minds were hardened, for until this day the same veil remains unlifted in the reading of the Old Testament...But even to this day, when Moses is read, a veil lies on their hearts* (2 Cor. 3:14-15).

When, however, the Lord returns to reign and they receive Him, *"the veil is taken away in Christ...when one turns to the Lord, the veil is taken away"* (2 Cor. 3:14, 16).

Tribulation with a purpose (Gen. 42-45)

Probably twenty-five years had passed since his brothers had thrown Joseph into the pit. Now began a period of trial and trouble for the ten men, designed to bring them to repentance and true confession. Joseph had probably already forgiven them in his heart, but he would not tell them they were forgiven until they confessed their sin.

All this presages the dispersion of the tribes of Israel and the seven years of tribulation, which they will endure before the Messiah returns to reign (Jer. 30:7; Mt. 24:3-31). He will deal with their consciences until they look on Him whom they pierced and mourn for Him as one mourns for an only son (Zech. 12:10).

There is great confusion today on the subject of forgiveness. A mother visits a prison and tells the convicted murderer of her daughter that she forgives him. Is that righteous? He has not confessed his sin nor asked for forgiveness. What is the proper scriptural procedure?

When a person has been wronged, he should forgive the culprit in his heart, but he does not tell him that he is forgiven. That might only encourage him in his wickedness. It seems to say that what he did was not serious.

The next step is to rebuke the offender. *"If your brother sins against you, rebuke him..."* (Lk. 17:3). The best way to do this is to show him from the Bible the wrong he has committed. The proper use of the law is to convict of sin (1 Tim. 1:8).

Not until the culprit repents does the offended one tell him that he is forgiven. *"If your brother sins against you, rebuke him; and **if he repents**, forgive him"* (Lk. 17:3).

We see Joseph following this order in his dealings with his brothers. He did not reveal himself to his brothers until they acknowledged their guilt.

People wrongfully conclude that when Jesus prayed *"Father, forgive them,"* His enemies were automatically forgiven. That is not so. Judas was not forgiven. The prayer covers only those who repented of their homicide.

Brother, yet unrecognized (Gen. 42:8)

When Joseph's brothers saw him on this first visit, they didn't recognize him. It is true that they were all twenty-five years older, but even so, you would think that there would be some glimmer of recognition. There must have been some trace of family likeness, some distinguishing feature that could have been a clue to his identity. Yet the Scriptures are silent on the subject. There is not the slightest suggestion that they suspected a blood relationship.

This clearly pictures the condition of the Jewish people at Christ's first advent. They rejected the Messiah even though He had legal rights to the throne of David through His genealogy (Mt. 1). They rejected Him even though He performed the miracles that were prophesied of the Messiah. They rejected Him even though many other messianic predictions found their fulfillment in Him.

In spite of all that, His Jewish brothers did not recognize Him. They did not accept Him as their Messiah. Because of this rejection, there is a veil over their eyes when they read the Old Testament (2 Cor. 3:14-15). They are judicially blinded, as predicted in Isaiah 6:9-10. It is a divine judgment on them.

When an individual Jew turns to the Lord, the veil is removed (2 Cor. 3:16), and the messianic Scriptures glow with meaning and splendor to him or her. But the veil will remain on the nation as a whole until the Lord returns in power and great glory.

Familiar faces (Gen. 42:8)

Though they had aged, the family likeness must have been still there. And possibly the Lord gave Joseph special powers of recognition. His brothers did not know him, but he knew them.

When Jesus came to earth, His people didn't realize who He truly was. He said to Philip, one of His earliest disciples, *"Have I been with you so long, and yet you have not known Me, Philip?"* But He knew them and He knew whether they were unbelievers or true sheep of His (Jn. 10:27). On one occasion He said to the Pharisees,

THE FIRST TRIP OF JOSEPH'S BROTHERS

"You know neither Me nor My Father" (Jn. 8:19). At another time He said to the people, *"But I know you..."* (Jn. 5:42).

Troubled consciences (Gen. 42:21)

First, Joseph's brothers bowed before him, just as he had predicted when he interpreted his dream (Gen. 37:8). Now notice his strategy in awakening their consciences.

When they asked to buy food, he accused them of being spies. They may well have accused him of being a spy (Gen. 37:17-18). In listing their family members, they said, *"The youngest is with our father today, and one is no more."* The mention of the youngest gave the governor the opportunity to insist that they bring Benjamin to him. The ambiguous comment *one is no more* gave him opportunity to play on that string also.

The governor ruled that one of the brothers should go and bring their youngest sibling while the others would stay in prison. This was enough to make their hearts sink. To tear Benjamin away from his father would be the death of Jacob. After they were in prison three days, the lord of Egypt changed the conditions. One of the brothers would remain in prison while the others would go to Canaan to get the youngest. The thought of taking Benjamin from their father who was still sorrowing over the loss of Joseph threw them into panic and confusion. Their pulses began to pound.

They had put him in a pit, possibly for three days. Their three-day confinement gave them time to associate their current troubles with what they had done to their brother.

The governor carefully crafted his strategy to awaken their memories, stab their consciences, and make them search for the reason for their calamities. "To arouse their dormant consciences, Joseph repeated as nearly as possible to them, their treatment of himself" (F. B. Meyer). The method was working. First, they acknowledged their guilt to one another:

> We are truly guilty concerning our brother, for we saw the anguish of his soul when he pleaded with us, and we would not hear; therefore this distress has come upon us (Gen. 42:21).

Blood-guiltiness (Gen. 42:22)

Reuben joined his brothers in acknowledging their guilt:

> Did I not speak to you, saying, "Do not sin against the boy; and you would not listen? Therefore his blood is now required of us" (Gen. 42:22).

His mention of blood-guiltiness has a sadly familiar sound. It reminds us of the angry mob who cried out to Pilate, *"His blood be upon us and on our children"* (Mt. 27:25).

His words also confirm a measure of repentance among the brothers. They prefigure the time when Israel will look on the Messiah whom they pierced and mourn for Him with deepest sorrow (Zech. 12:10).

No secrets (Gen. 42:23)

They probably thought that the governor was a pure-blooded Egyptian who didn't understand Hebrew. After all, he had used an interpreter. But he clearly understood them when he heard them talking among themselves. He heard their private confession of the outrageous way they had treated him.

Our Lord also knew what was said in secret. When the disciples reasoned among themselves about leaven, He knew what they were saying (Mt. 16:7-8). When the scribes privately agreed that the Lord committed blasphemy because He forgave sins, He knew every word (Mk. 2:8). At other times He even knew what they were thinking (Mt. 12:14-15, 25; 27:18; Lk. 6:8; 9:46-47).

Mercy and grace (Gen. 42:25)

In spite of the fact that Joseph spoke roughly to them (Gen. 42:7), he provided them with grain, money, and provisions for the journey. Simeon, often rated as one of the most cruel, was left in prison, while the others started the journey home. Remember that Simeon was the oldest brother there when Joseph was sold to the Midianites.

Joseph's abundant provision for them reminds us of the generosity of the Lord Jesus Christ. Though He was rich, He became poor for our sakes so that we might become rich (2 Cor. 8:9).

On the trip home, one brother found his money in his pack. Disquieting, to say the least. Would the governor now accuse him of stealing? But it was even more distressing when the rest of them emptied their packs back at home and found their money also. This cast doubt on their protestations of being honest men. The ruler's strategy to bring them to repentance continued to work.

Tension arose still further when they told Jacob that Benjamin must go back with them. The governor had insisted on that. The old man reacted as they knew he would; he was stricken with grief. He refused to give up the youngest. Reuben promised to guarantee Benjamin's return, offering the lives of his own two sons as penalty for failure. But it was no use. Jacob's mind was steel. It was only when the famine became more severe and when Judah offered himself as a surety for Benjamin, that Jacob yielded, and then only grudgingly.

The old patriarch sent fruits, nuts, balm, honey, and spices to the Egyptian governor. As for the returned money, he doubled it.

The Hound of Heaven was relentlessly pursuing the brothers.

Chapter Five

THE SECOND TRIP OF JOSEPH'S BROTHERS TO EGYPT

The only way (Gen. 41:55)

In the famine-stricken world, Joseph was the only way of salvation. He was the only hope, the only source of life-sustaining bread.

Here he is a perfect picture of the Lord Jesus, who said, *"I am the way, the truth, and the life. No one comes to the Father except through Me"* (Jn. 14:6).

Peter likewise reminds us:

Nor is there salvation in any other, for there is no other name under heaven given among men by which we must be saved (Acts 4:12).

For no other foundation can anyone lay than that which is laid, which is Jesus Christ (1 Cor. 3:11).

Today people think it is narrow-minded to say that Christ is the only way to God. But arguing against it doesn't change the fact. If we could have been saved in any other way, then be sure that God would not have sent His Son to die for us. He would not have paid the greatest price if a lesser price would do. If we could have been saved in any other way, then Christ needlessly sacrificed His life (Gal. 2:21).

Come to the feast (Gen. 43:16)

When the governor saw his brothers and Benjamin, he ordered a feast to be spread for them. He sat alone at one table. The brothers sat by themselves at another table. And the Egyptians sat by themselves also. That is a curious twist: The Hebrews were an abomination to the Egyptians. Customarily the Gentiles were the ones who were looked down on by the Jews.

The brothers misunderstood the governor's motives and intentions, thinking he was going to punish them for the money in their packs. So they made a long explanation to the steward, protesting their innocence in the matter. He assured them they had nothing to fear.

So it will be with the nation of Israel in a coming day. The Messiah will not refuse them or cast them out. He is not through with His ancient, earthly people. The promises to Abraham must be fulfilled. In the meantime He waits that He might be gracious to Israel (Isa. 30:18).

Dreams fulfilled (Gen. 43:23-26)

After Joseph ordered Simeon to be released from

prison, the brothers met the governor and bowed before him in fulfillment of his dreams twenty-five years earlier. They doubtlessly thought of sheaves and stars. Joseph saw the gears of God meshing. He realized that events were sparkling with the supernatural. The denouement was near.

This anticipates the time when a remnant of Israel will acknowledge the Lord Jesus to be their Messiah-Savior. Perhaps we already see this glorious climax approaching as an unprecedented number of Jewish people are turning to Yeshua as their Messiah. More have done this in the last few years than in the previous 1900 years.

Tears of joy (Gen. 43:30)

Overcome with emotion, especially to see Benjamin, Joseph sought a private place where he could weep. There are seven other times when we see him weeping. The first one occurred when he heard his brothers agreeing among themselves how wrongly they had treated him (Gen. 42:24). The others are: when they took their second trip to Egypt and Joseph was about to reveal his identity to them (Gen. 45:2); when he embraced Benjamin (Gen. 45:14); when he kissed the other brothers (Gen. 45:15); when his father Jacob died (Gen. 50:1); and finally when his brothers asked him to forgive them (Gen. 50:17).

Centuries later, the Man of Sorrows wept at the grave of Lazarus (Jn. 11:35). He wept over the city of Jerusalem saying, *"I would but you would not"* (Lk. 19:41; Mt. 23:37). And He wept in the garden of Gethsemane, as Hebrews 5:7 states:

Who, in the days of His flesh, when He had offered up prayers and
supplications, with vehement cries and tears to Him who was able
to save from death, and was heard because of His godly fear.

The garden is not explicitly mentioned here, so it is possible that His sufferings on the cross are also in view.

At the banquet table, the governor seated them according to their ages. The men were astonished. How could he know who was the oldest, and all the way down to the youngest? It seemed that nothing was hidden from him.

Benjamin's food serving was five times bigger than the others (Gen. 43:34). Later Benjamin would get five sets of new clothes and 300 pieces of silver, perhaps five times as much money (Gen. 45:22). They had previously resented Joseph's preferential treatment; now they would see Benjamin enjoying more of everything. Would this reminder of their past envy prick their consciences? And would their jealousy be gone?

Even more astonishing than the way the governor seated them will be the Messiah's ability to sort out the tribes of Israel, long scattered among the Gentile nations. At His Second Advent, He will regather the Jews from Ethiopia, the Chinese Jews of Kaifeng-Fu, the Cochin Jews from India, and Jews from Japan and other countries until all twelve tribes are restored to their homeland.

The final trial (Gen. 44:6-34)

Dark clouds lay ahead on the journey home! The governor had arranged to have his silver cup stowed in Benjamin's sack. Then after the fellows had started for home, he ordered his steward to overtake them and accuse them of stealing it. He suggested that their conduct was small thanks for all the kindness that he had shown to them.

The brothers protested complete innocence and rashly blurted that if the steward found the cup in one of the sacks, the culprit should die and the rest of them should be Pharaoh's slaves. It was a rash vow.

The search began, from the sack of the oldest down to Benjamin's. Imagine their mounting terror as the search slowly eliminated Reuben, Simeon, Levi, Judah, Zebulun, Issachar, Dan, Gad, Asher, Naphtali. Only Benjamin was left. Sure enough, the steward found the governor's silver goblet, which he had secretly planted in Benjamin's sack. He said it was the cup that the governor used for divining.

This was a form of fortune telling by the aid of supernatural powers. For example: The psychic might float some oil in water and then interpret the shape and movement of the oil. Divination was later forbidden by the law of God (Deut. 18:10-11).

This was the worst thing that could happen, the worst possible scenario. It might mean that Benjamin would die (Gen. 44:9), that the brothers would be slaves (44:9), that Reuben's two sons would die (42:37), that Judah would bear lifelong blame, having failed as a surety (43:9), and that Jacob would go down to the grave in sorrow (42:38).

The divining cup (Gen. 44:5)
Many Christians arch their eyebrows when they read

that Joseph practiced divination with a silver cup. What is an occultic practice like this doing in the Word of God?

It is important to remember that the brothers thought that the governor (their brother) was an Egyptian, and it would be usual for such a pagan official to have a divining cup to discover secrets. Already the ruler had displayed remarkable knowledge of these fellows from Canaan. How did he know? Perhaps his silver cup was a prop to provide them with a natural explanation. But did that cup have a dark side too? Could the governor use it to find out the way they had treated their missing brother? Would this be a way for their sins to find them out?

The Lord Jesus needs no divining cup. He is all knowing. To Him our lives are an open book. *"All things are naked and open to the eyes of Him to whom we must give account"* (Heb. 4:13).

> Though infinitely glorious and gloriously grand,
> He knows the eternal story of every grain of sand.

Two cups are prominent in Jesus' life. Of one He said, *"Shall I not drink the cup which My Father has given Me?"* (Jn. 18:11). That was His sufferings and death at Calvary. The other is the cup that symbolizes the New Covenant in His blood, shed for us (Lk. 22:20).

Returning to the city, the brothers prostrated themselves before the governor and pled for mercy. The governor's judgment was tempered with compassion. He ruled that Benjamin would be his slave and the rest of them could go home.

Then acting as surety, Judah made a clean breast of the

whole story. Sir Walter Scott said that this speech was "the most complete pattern of genuine natural eloquence extant in any language."

First Judah rehearsed the events that had brought Benjamin to Egypt. The governor had asked if the brothers had a father or a brother. They had said that they had an aged father, a young brother (Benjamin), and that another brother (Joseph) was dead. (Little did Judah realize that he was talking to the "dead" brother.) The father was especially fond of Benjamin because he was the only surviving child of Rachel.

Judah continued. When the governor had previously insisted that Benjamin must come to Egypt, the brothers had protested that this might precipitate the death of their father. Previously, they had been insensitive to his feelings and those of their brother Joseph. Now that was all changed. There was deep affection and concern.

The governor had been adamant. Benjamin must come or they would get no more help in Egypt. They would never see the governor again. So they had returned to Canaan and had broken the news to Jacob. This had thrown the aged patriarch into panic. He reminded them that his wife Rachel had borne two sons and that an animal probably killed one of them. Judah told all this to the governor. The "dead" son is listening to his own "obituary." Jacob had said that if they took Benjamin from him, he would go to his grave in sorrow. In love for their father, the brothers had pled for Benjamin.

Judah told how the impasse was broken when he offered to serve as surety for his young brother. If

Benjamin did not return to his father, Judah would bear the blame.

Having finished a review of how Benjamin came to Egypt, Judah offered himself as a slave in place of his youngest brother if the governor would let Benjamin go. Erdman notes:

> They had been cruel, heartless, jealous, violent; now they were willing to die for one another. They had once broken their father's heart with the blood-stained robe. Now they had come to have real love and tender sympathy for the aged patriarch.[11]

Judah's confession was genuine. He did not try to make excuses, to shift blame, to gloss over their wickedness, or to withhold the truth without telling a lie. His was the true repentance that Christ demands, the godly repentance that leads to salvation (2 Cor. 7:10). Before there can be reconciliation, there has to be full, heartfelt, and sorrowful repentance.

Judah's role as surety reminds us of Christ's suretyship. Judah offered himself as a guarantee. He would be a slave in Benjamin's place so that Benjamin could go back to his father.

The Lord Jesus is a Surety in a somewhat different sense. He is the Surety of a new and better covenant (Heb. 7:22). The old covenant was the law. It was weak in that it told Israel what to do but did not give the people the power to do it. The new covenant tells what God will do. The old covenant was written on tablets of stone. The new covenant will be placed in the minds of the people and written in their hearts. In other words they will be disposed to obey the Lord, not through fear of punishment but through love for the Lord.

For this is the covenant that I will make with the house of Israel: After those days, says the Lord, I will put My laws in their mind, and write them on their hearts, and I will be their God, and they shall be My people (Heb. 8:10).

Notice that the new covenant is made primarily with the house of Israel. However, believers today enjoy some of its benefits:

For I will be merciful to their unrighteousness, and their sins and their lawless deeds I will remember no more (Heb. 8:12).

The Lord Jesus is Surety in the sense that He will bring to pass all that is promised in the new covenant. This will take place at the Second Advent, when Israel turns to the Lord and enjoys His millennial reign.

Up until now, the brothers had been dogged with one trial after another. Calamity followed calamity. It was "as though a man fled from a lion, and a bear met him; or as though he went into the house, leaned his hand on the wall, and a serpent bit him" (Amos 5:19). God was

...like a lion to Ephraim, and like a young lion to the house of Judah. I, even I, will tear them and go away; I will take them away, and no one shall rescue (Hos. 5:14).

He is waiting for them to say,

Come, and let us return to the Lord, for He has torn, but He will heal us; He has stricken, but He will bind us up (Hos. 6:1).

Think of some of the things that had aroused their consciences:

• When Joseph accused them of being spies (Gen. 42:9), they were reminded of how they had resented his "spying" on them (Gen. 42:11).

• They said, *"We are honest men."* Really? Then why did they lie to their father about Joseph's disappearance?

In introducing themselves to Joseph, they said, *"One is no more"* (Gen. 42:13, 32). They must have swallowed hard at this point.

• Joseph put them in prison for three days (Gen. 42:17). This was designed to remind them how they had "imprisoned" Joseph in a pit.

• Joseph demanded that they bring back their youngest brother when they returned from Canaan (Gen. 42:20, 34). Benjamin was now closest to his father's heart, the position once held by Joseph.

• When they returned to get Benjamin, they were horrified to find in their baggage the money that they had used to buy grain (Gen. 42:27, 35). This made them look like crooks, not honest men.

• On the return to Canaan, Benjamin found the divining cup in his sack (Gen. 44:12).

Hasn't this been the history of the nation of Israel, one crisis following another? No people have ever suffered so much as God's ancient, earthly people. But a better day is coming when *"all Israel will be saved, as it is written: The Deliverer will come out of Zion, and He will turn away ungodliness from Jacob"* (Rom. 11:26).

Chapter Six

JOSEPH REVEALS HIS IDENTITY

Come near (Gen. 45:1)

The tribulation is past. The governor's stratagem was successful. The brothers have repented. Confession has restored fellowship.

On their second visit, the governor commanded everyone but his brothers to leave the room. There must be no mediator, no one to share the work of reconciliation. Alone there with his brothers, he could restrain himself no longer. He broke out in loud crying, loud enough to be heard in the rest of the palace. That must have seemed strange to the brothers. Why was this Egyptian governor wailing? Then he revealed himself to them and told them to come near. It is one of the most moving scenes in all of Scripture, a classic case of emotional overload. Unwearied in forgiveness, Joseph's heart could only love.

What a picture of Christ, the Redeemer! After centuries of rejection by His own people, He will reveal

Himself to them in pure grace. It will be His work and His alone. All day long He has stretched out His hands to a disobedient and contrary people (Rom. 10:21), yet He longs to make Himself known to them as their Messiah-King and Eternal Lover. *"Come to Me,"* He says, *"all you who labor, and are heavy laden, and I will give you rest"* (Mt. 11:28). Through Isaiah, He invites, *"Ho! Everyone who thirsts, come to the waters; and you who have no money, come, buy and eat. Yes, come, buy wine and milk without money and without price"* (Isa. 55:1).

The whole world will be speechless when they see Him in all His glory.

So shall He sprinkle many nations. Kings shall shut their mouths at Him; for what had not been told them they shall see, and what they had not heard they shall consider (Isa. 52:15).

Of course, we can also make an application to the Rapture when we, the bride of Christ, meet Him whom having not seen we love. What a moment that will be!

> Glorious day when we stand in His presence,
> When all our heartaches and sorrows are past,
> When earth's best beauties fade as a flower,
> We shall see Jesus at last.

An unknown poet exults when he thinks of that first glimpse of the Lord Jesus:

> Not merely one glimpse but forever,
> At home with Him ever to be,
> At home in the glory celestial
> Where shimmers the crystal sea.

> But there, even there in that glory
> Will anything ever efface
> That rapturous moment of moments,
> My first, first look at His face.

We shall see the eternal Son of God who died for us. He won't have to say, *"I am Jesus."* We will recognize Him right away. We will see the marks of Calvary in His hands, feet, and side. We'll hear His well-known voice. The glorified Man will tell us to draw near. We will fall at His feet and worship Him without hindrance. To be with Him and like Him for all eternity will be the heaven of heavens for us.

Dumbfounded (Gen. 45:3)

Joseph's brothers were dumbfounded, too awestruck to speak. This would always rank as one of the greatest days in their lives. They would never forget the moment when they heard the words, *"I am Joseph; does my father still live?"*

The announcement triggered a wide gamut of emotions. It stunned them to realize that their brother was now the governor of Egypt. The sibling they had abandoned to die was not only alive; he was crowned with glory and honor. By what strange set of circumstances did their brother Joseph rise to such eminence?

As they gazed on him, they began to see the family likeness. It was as if a veil had lifted from their eyes. Then guilt and shame swept over them. They had plotted his death, had thrown him into a cistern, and had forsaken him. Guilt changed to fear. What would he do to them, now that he was in the position of power?

Joy mingled with wonder. Suddenly they found themselves loving Joseph. No longer was there a trace of envy in their hearts. Once they were jealous of his coat of many colors. Now they were proud to see him the second-best dressed man in the realm.

Joseph acted swiftly to quell their anxious emotions by tracing the signature of a sovereign God in all that happened since they had last seen one another.

Reconciled at last (Gen. 45:4)

When Joseph invited his brothers to draw near and they responded, there was true reconciliation. Their hostility was gone. They were no longer estranged or cut off. Barriers to fellowship were torn down. Joseph didn't need to be reconciled. He had never ceased to love them. They were the ones whose wickedness had cut them off from their brother.

This has an application for today. Men and women need to be reconciled to God. As soon as they draw near to Him in faith, the conflict is ended, and they have peace with God through the Lord Jesus Christ.

The scene in Genesis 45:4 also looks forward to the time when Israel will look on Him whom they nailed to a cross of wood and grieve for Him with intense mourning (Zech. 12:10).

The Lord still says to His own, *"Draw near."* It is our privilege and duty to *"draw near with a true heart in full assurance of faith, having our hearts sprinkled from an*

JOSEPH REVEALS HIS IDENTITY

evil conscience, and our bodies washed with pure water"
(Heb. 10:22).

Good out of evil (Gen. 45:5,7)

Joseph's brothers had resented him and sold him. Their behavior was a catalog of maltreatment. Anyone's natural reaction would have been to cherish the anger that seeks revenge. But Joseph was not vindictive. He was able to trace the overruling hand of God in it all. His reassuring words to his guilty brothers are remarkable.

> *I am Joseph your brother, whom you sold into Egypt. But now, do not therefore be grieved or angry with yourselves because you sold me here; for God sent me before you to preserve life...And God sent me before you to preserve a posterity for you, and to save your lives by a great deliverance. So now it was not you who sent me here, but God* (Gen. 45:4-5, 7-8).

The Lord Jesus had been scorned, vilified, insulted, and beaten. He *"endured such hostility of sinners against Himself"* (Heb. 12:3). Yet when facing towering rejection and unbelief, He could say, *"Even so, Father, for so it seemed good in Your sight"* (Mt. 11:26). This confidence delivered Him from being vindictive.

J. N. Darby could have been thinking of Joseph's history when he wrote,

> God is behind the scenes, but He moves all the scenes which He is behind. We have to learn this, and let Him work, and not think much of man's busy movements; they will accomplish God's. The rest of them all perish and disappear. We have only peacefully to do His will.

Lord of all (Gen. 45:8)

Joseph told his brothers, *"God has made me lord of all Egypt."* From the human standpoint, it was Pharaoh who had promoted him to that office, but Joseph was able to see God's role in all the circumstances of his life.

In like manner God gave the Lord Jesus power over all flesh (Jn. 17:4). He highly exalted His Son and gave Him the name of highest honor (Phil. 2:9). He has *"put all things under His feet and has given Him to be head over all things to the Church"* (Eph. 1:22). This means more than that He is the Head of the Church. It means that the Head of the Church is Head over all things, the Ruler of the universe.

A great commission (Gen. 45:9)

Joseph now said to his brothers,

> *Hasten and go up to my father, and say to him, "Thus says your son Joseph: 'God has made me lord of all Egypt; come down to me, do not tarry.'"*

Those brothers had never been sent on such a thrilling mission, and their old father Jacob had never heard such good news.

Just prior to His ascension, the risen Savior left this commission with His disciples:

> *Go therefore and make disciples of all the nations, baptizing them in the name of the Father and of the Son and of the Holy Spirit, teaching them to observe all things that I have commanded you, and lo, I am with you always, even to the end of the age* (Mt. 28:20).

Those are our standing orders, but they also have an application to the future. Christ's Jewish brothers during the Tribulation will go forth to proclaim that He is alive, that He is the true Messiah, and the Savior of mankind. They will preach the gospel of the kingdom, namely, that salvation is by faith in the Lord Jesus and that those who believe will enter the millennium with Him.

No distance now (Gen. 45:10)

The entire family with all their possessions would dwell in the land of Goshen and be near Joseph. Goshen was not far from the royal palace.

That makes us think of how Jesus prayed that believers, given by the Father, would be with Him in heaven (Jn. 17:24), and He promised that it would be so: *"Where I am, there you may be also"* (Jn. 14:3). Gerhard Tersteegen rejoiced:

> He and I, in that bright glory
> One deep joy shall share;
> Mine to be forever with Him,
> His that I am there.

All your need (Gen. 45:11)

Joseph was determined that none of his family would ever come to poverty. He would supply all their needs when they came to Goshen:

> *There I will provide for you, lest you and your household, and all that you have, come to poverty; for there are still five years of famine* (Gen. 45:11).

And so it is that Christ's "brothers" have the promise, *"And my God shall supply all your need according to His riches in glory by Christ Jesus"* (Phil. 4:19). If we are supplied according to His riches in glory, we will be abundantly cared for. There should be no room for worry or for fear.

Jesus promised that if we seek first the kingdom of God and His righteousness, He will provide us with the necessities of life (Mt. 6:33). *"Having food and clothing, with these we shall be content"* (1 Tim. 6:8).

All his glory (Gen. 45:13)

When his brothers were leaving to bring their father to Egypt, Joseph said, *"So you shall tell my Father of all my glory in Egypt, and of all that you have seen"* (Gen. 45:13).

We have a counterpart privilege and responsibility in our lives today. As we come to God in worship, we should extol the glories of His beloved Son, the glories of His deity, humanity, cross, resurrection, ascension, and position in heaven. Especially when we gather for the Breaking of Bread we should tell the Father of all the Savior's excellencies. God knows the honors of His Son better than we do, but He loves to hear us expressing our appreciation of Him.

Kisses of reconciliation (Gen. 45:15)

When Joseph kissed them, they knew it was a middle-eastern expression of deep affection and, in this case, of full and free forgiveness. They had nothing to fear.

A moment more saw him and Benjamin locked in each other's arms, their tears flowing freely. And he kissed all his brethren. Simeon? Yes. Reuben? Yes. Those who had tied his hands and mocked his cries? Yes. He kissed them all. And after that they talked with him.

So it shall be one day. The Jews are slowly filtering back to the land in unbelief. Sore troubles await them there, to prepare them to recognize their rejected Messiah. But the time is not far distant when they shall be prepared to hear Him say, "I am Jesus, your brother, whom you crucified; but be not grieved with yourselves, for God has brought good out of evil, both for Gentile and for Jew, by saving life with a great deliverance." *"And they shall look upon Him whom they pierced, and mourn because of Him." "And so all* [believing] *Israel shall be saved"* [12]

They talked with him (Gen. 45:15)

After Joseph kissed them, they talked with him. It was not incidental. Fellowship follows forgiveness. Sin had broken fellowship between the brothers and Joseph. The kiss of forgiveness and reconciliation assured them that all was forgiven. Now they are free to converse with him, and probably on better terms than they had ever known before.

At the present time Israel is not on talking terms with the Messiah. The nation is cast aside. Diplomatic relations have been broken. But when a remnant turns to the Lord, He will forgive their sins and iniquities and remember them no more. He will write the law on their hearts and put a new Spirit in them.

Great among the nations (Gen. 45:16)

After the governor revealed his identity to his brothers, "the report of it was heard in Pharaoh's house" and rejoicing erupted in the palace. Pharaoh and his servants were pleased.

So it is when a sinner repents, there is rejoicing in the presence of the angels in heaven. And so it will be at the Second Coming of Christ. The Messiah's fame will be known among the Gentiles. *"The Gentiles will come to Your light, and kings to the brightness of Your rising"* (Isa. 60:3).

> *Now it shall come to pass in the latter days that the mountain of the Lord's house shall be established on the top of the mountains, and shall be exalted above the hills; and peoples shall flow to it. Many nations shall come and say, "Come, and let us go up to the mountain of the Lord, to the house of the God of Jacob; He will teach us His ways, and we shall walk in His paths." For out of Zion the law shall go forth, and the word of the Lord from Jerusalem* (Micah 4:1-2).

> *For from the rising of the sun, even to its going down, My name shall be great among the Gentiles; in every place incense shall be offered to My name, and a pure offering; For My name shall be great among the nations, says the Lord of hosts* (Mal. 1:11).

He commissioned them (Gen. 45:17)

Joseph sent his brothers back to Canaan bearing a great commission and heralding good news. They were to go to their father and tell him that Joseph was alive (Gen. 45:4); that God had made him lord of all Egypt (Gen.

45:8); and that their father and the rest of the family should pack up and move to Egypt (Gen. 45:9).

So God will commission redeemed Israel to carry the message of deliverance to the entire world. God's ancient people will be a channel of blessing to every nation as they tell of all the glories of the Lord Jesus.

We too are commissioned to tell of all Christ's glory—the fact that He rose and lives in the power of an endless life, that He has been exalted in heaven, and that He is glorified at God's right hand. Ours is the gospel of the glory of Christ. As royal priests we go forth to proclaim the excellencies of Him who called us out of darkness into His marvelous light (1 Pet. 2:9). Like Peter we preach *"peace through Jesus Christ—He is Lord of all"* (Acts 10:36).

Twice Joseph told his brothers to hurry (45:9, 13). We too should hasten. Souls are dying. Over half the world has never heard of man's only hope. There is no time for trivia. "There is no time to while away the hours. All must be earnest in a world like ours."

> The work that centuries might have done
> Must crowd the hours of setting sun.

Blest with the best (Gen. 45:18, 20)

Because of their relationship to Joseph, his brothers received the best of the land of Egypt. Goshen was the garden spot of that land, and it was all theirs.

This corresponds to the spiritual wealth that Christ's "brothers" inherit. They have life more abundantly (Jn.

10:10). As heirs of God and joint heirs with Christ, they inherit all things (1 Cor. 3:22; Rom. 8:17). They have joy, peace, hope, rest, and freedom. They possess a new purpose in life and are satisfied with Jesus. As recipients of eternal life, they are forgiven, redeemed, and saved. As to their standing before God, they are justified, sanctified, accepted in the Beloved, complete in Christ, and loved as Christ is loved. The Holy Spirit indwells, baptizes, seals, guarantees, and anoints them.

Every believer is a child of God, a priest, and more than a conqueror. He or she is blessed with all spiritual blessings in the heavenlies. We are the most privileged people in the world. No doubt about it.

An added share (Gen. 45:22)

In providing for their trip home, Joseph gave Benjamin 300 pieces of silver (15 times what the brothers received for Joseph when they sold him!) and five changes of clothing—more than the others (Gen. 45:22).

So the Lord Jesus has provided for us super-abundantly. He has promised to supply all our needs according to His riches in glory (Phil. 4:19). All things are ours, and we are His, and He is God's (1 Cor. 3:22-23). His grace is sufficient (2 Cor. 12:9). We have all things that pertain to life and godliness (2 Pet. 1:3). We can never be poor.

Good news (Gen. 45:25-28)

Home at last after the long, hot journey from Egypt! As soon as the wagons drive into the front yard, the fellows jump off and burst through the door. There is no time for the usual greetings. A cacophony of voices startles the aged patriarch. All the men are speaking at the same time in breathless, staccato bursts. When Jacob manages to call for order, then the reason for the excitement becomes clear. "Joseph is alive, Dad. We saw him. We talked to him and he talked to us. He is the number two man in Egypt. Dad, he asked for you. The whole thing is incredible. You should see the magnificence in which he lives. He is handsome. And he was so kind to us."

For years Jacob had the evidence of the bloodied coat of many colors to convince him that Joseph was dead. Now he is stunned to hear that his favorite son is alive in Egypt. It seemed too good to be true. It's a wonder that the news did not induce cardiac arrest in the old man.

In like manner, the news of Christ's resurrection sent shock waves throughout Judea. An angel told the two Marys at the empty tomb:

> Do not be afraid, for I know that you seek Jesus who was crucified. He is not here; for He is risen, as He said. Come, see the place where the Lord lay (Mt. 28:5-6).

The disciples went forth to proclaim a risen Savior: at Pentecost Peter thundered, *"God raised* [Him] *up, having loosed the pains of death"* (Acts 2:24).

A problem (Gen. 45:26)

The news that Joseph was still alive put the brothers in an embarrassing position. How could they explain his continued existence without condemning themselves for their sinfulness? They had told their father that a beast had probably devoured him, literally torn him to pieces. Now they had to tell him that his beloved son was alive.

Just as Joseph's preservation posed a problem to his brothers, so the resurrection of the Lord Jesus put His assailants in a difficult position. How could they explain the empty tomb? As we have seen, the religious leaders bribed the military guard to say that Christ's disciples came at night and stole His body (Mt. 28:12-13).

Where there is true conversion, there is no resistance to being exposed. True confession does not hide or excuse sin. It makes a clean break with the past and marvels at the grace that can forgive such a weight of sin.

Chapter Seven

JACOB'S MOVE TO EGYPT

When Jacob saw the carts that had brought his sons back from Egypt and the provisions that Joseph had sent, he believed that Joseph was still alive. He finally agreed to go to see his beloved son.

On the way he stopped at Beersheba on the edge of the Negev (desert) to offer sacrifices to the Lord. There God appeared to him with a message of encouragement. He should not fear to go to Egypt. The Lord would go with him, would make of him a great nation, and would bring him back to Canaan (see Gen. 50:7-14). Joseph would put his hand on Jacob's eyes, that is, he would close his father's eyes in death.

With that assurance, Jacob set out with his extended family of seventy, his livestock, and his other possessions. With Judah as a guiding scout, they came to the land of Goshen.

Grace is free (Gen. 42, 43, 47)

The first time the brothers had gone to Egypt, they took money to buy grain, but Joseph ordered his servants to give them freely the grain they wanted, to restore their money, and to provide for their trip home (Gen. 42:25-26). The word *buy* occurs five times in the first ten verses of Genesis 42. But everything was free. Because grace is free, we are invited to come and buy without money and without price (Isa. 55:1).

On their second trip to Egypt, Joseph's brothers took double money plus the money that had been refunded the first time plus fruits, balm, and honey (Gen. 43:11-12). Again Joseph ordered his steward to give them grain without cost and to refund their money and gifts of food.

When Jacob's family finally moved to Egypt with all their possessions, Joseph gave them the best of the land and all the bread they needed. There was no mention of their having to pay for it (Gen. 47:11-12). There was no thought of earning it or deserving it. It was pure grace.

Instead of accepting God's righteousness by grace through faith, Israel has tried to establish their own righteousness (Rom. 10:3). They did not seek righteousness by faith but by the works of the law (Rom. 9:32).

Like Joseph's brothers, natural man thinks he can earn salvation by good works or merit it by good character. But eternal life is a gift to those who deserve the opposite. When a person comes to Christ as a guilty, lost sinner and receives Him as the only way of salvation, the Lord Jesus showers Him with the riches of His grace. Joseph typifies Jesus in this as he does in so many ways.

Chapter Eight

THE FAMILY REUNITED

A distinct people (Gen. 46:28)

When Joseph heard that his aged father had come as far as Goshen, he hurried to meet him. It was a gala reunion. He fell on his father's neck and wept a good while. Israel (Jacob) was overjoyed. He felt that life could have no greater rapture than to be with Joseph, his long lost son, so he said he was ready to die.

Then Joseph worked out a strategy to secure Goshen as a property for his family. After taking his relatives to the palace, he told Pharaoh that his father and family had arrived and he was careful to mention that they were shepherds. That was the crucial word. Before presenting five of his brothers to Pharaoh, he prompted them to be sure to use the word *shepherds*. Again the pivotal word. Since shepherds were an abomination to the Egyptians, it was desirable to segregate them, and Goshen, the finest pastureland, proved to be the place chosen. Why did the

Egyptians have contempt for shepherds? Perhaps it was because they did not value sheep for food or sacrifice, and the senseless behavior of the animals did not command admiration or respect. Because shepherds are associated with sheep, they were at the bottom of the social ladder.

Unashamed (Gen. 47:2)

Joseph's brothers were country hicks who spoke a foreign language and knew nothing of royal etiquette. Even if instructed by Joseph, they probably felt very uneasy in the court of a Gentile king, and looked completely out of place. Yet Joseph was not ashamed to present five of his brothers to Pharaoh.

By nature we were neither wise, powerful, nor noble. Instead we were foolish, weak, base, nobodies. In spite of all that, the Lord Jesus is not ashamed to call us *"brothers"* (Heb. 2:11). Nor will He be ashamed of us when we reach the eternal dwellings and He introduces us to the sovereign God. Did He not promise, *"Whoever confesses Me before men, him I will also confess before My Father who is in heaven"* (Mt. 10:32)? Just think of that!

Jacob blesses Pharaoh (Gen. 47:10)

Jacob brought his father to meet Pharaoh. The aged patriarch blessed the ruler, both before and at the close of the interview (vv. 7, 10). Pharaoh started by asking Jacob his age. The Hebrew answered:

> *The days of the years of my pilgrimage are one hundred and thirty years; few and evil have been the days of the years of my life,*

and they have not attained to the days of the years of the life of my fathers in the days of their pilgrimage.

It is regrettable that in one of the happiest periods of his existence, Jacob should have felt it necessary to complain. It would have been a good opportunity to witness to the love, grace, and mercy of the God of Abraham and Isaac. But who are we to criticize when we think of opportunities to witness that we have missed?

Now watch Jacob pronouncing a blessing on the ruler. A wrinkled, unimposing Jew blessing a ruler in magnificent attire. But wait a minute. The writer to the Hebrews reminds us that *"beyond all contradiction the lesser is blessed by the better"* (Heb. 7:7). Pharaoh was the lesser and Jacob the better. This may not be man's way of seeing things, but it is God's.

Separation (Gen. 47:11)

In spite of hesitation and fear, Jacob settled in Goshen. The tribes were thus providentially separated from the rest of Egypt. God had always wanted Israel to be *"a people dwelling alone, not reckoning itself among the nations"* (Num. 23:9). He wanted to preserve them from the contamination of idolatry.

Our heavenly Joseph wants His people today to be separate. They are in the world but not of it (Jn. 17:14). Christ was not *"of the world"* at all, and He is the model for us. We are an abomination to the people of the world, or, as Paul said, we are *"as the filth of the world, the offscouring of all things"* (1 Cor. 4:13). We should be happy to have it so. Get used to it, Christian!

We are but strangers here, we do not crave
A home on earth, which gave Thee but a grave:
Thy cross has severed ties which bound us here,
Thyself our treasure in a brighter sphere.

—J. G. Deck

Total commitment (Gen. 47:25)

Joseph then turned his attention to dealing with the famine. When it became extreme in Egypt, he provided the people with food in exchange for livestock. He bought the land and provided seed for planting with the understanding that 20% of the crop would go to the government. The people responded, *"You have saved our lives; let us find favor in the sight of my lord, and we will be Pharaoh's servants."*

The New Testament counterpart of this is that we should present all that we have and are to the One who has saved us by a great deliverance. Like the Hebrew slave we should say, *"I love my Master; I will not go out free."* We should present our bodies a living sacrifice, holy, acceptable to God—our reasonable service (Rom. 12:1). As Isaac Watts wrote, "Love so amazing, so divine demands my heart, my life, my all."

First the natural, then the spiritual (Gen. 48)

Genesis 48 has the interesting ceremony of Israel's (Jacob's) blessing Joseph's two sons. Joseph thought it was a mistake when his sight-impaired father set Ephraim, the younger, before Manasseh. When he objected, his father said, in effect, "No, this is the way it should be." He was right. Often in God's providence, the younger gets precedence over the older. So we see Abel over Cain, Isaac over Ishmael, Jacob over Esau, and Joseph over Reuben.

But even more to the point we see Jesus over Adam:

> *And so it is written, "The first man Adam became a living being." The last Adam became a life-giving spirit...The first man was of the earth, made of dust; the second Man is the Lord from heaven* (1 Cor. 15:45-47).

The father beloved

Joseph loved his father passionately. On his brothers' first two trips to Egypt, he was frequently inquiring about his dad. *"Is your father still alive?"* (Gen. 43:7). *"Is your father well, the old man of whom you spoke? Is he still alive?"* (Gen. 43:27). After making himself known to his brothers, Joseph said,

> *Hasten and go up to my father, and say to him, "Thus says your son Joseph: 'God has made me lord of all Egypt, come down to me, do not tarry'"* (Gen. 45:9).

When Jacob finally arrived, Joseph went to Goshen to meet him (Gen. 46:29). Later he introduced his father to Pharaoh (Gen. 47:7), provided him with all necessities (Gen. 47:12), and vowed to honor his desire to be buried in Canaan (Gen. 47:29-31). When Jacob died, Joseph *"fell on his father's face, and wept over him, and kissed him"* (Gen. 50:1).

After mourning seven days, Joseph traveled with that precious body to its resting-place in the Cave of

Machpelah in Hebron (Gen. 50:13-14). There is no record of Joseph's ever saying he loved his father, but his actions spoke louder than words.

The life of the Lord Jesus was an unbroken record of doing the will of His Father. He submitted to His Father's plan, obeyed the Father's commands. There was never an act of self-will. Only once did He say He loved His Father. That was in John 14:31,

> But that the world may know that I love the Father, and as the Father gave Me commandment, so do I.

The next day He demonstrated the immensity of that love by going to the cross and dying for sinners in obedience to His Father.

> No man of greater love can boast
> Than for his friend to die.
> Christ for His enemies was slain;
> What love with His can vie?
> —*Joseph Stennett*

Chapter Nine

THE PATRIARCHAL BLESSING

Jacob's blessing of Joseph (Gen. 49:22-26)
Now we come to Jacob's blessings on his twelve sons. Here is what he said about Joseph:

> *Joseph is a fruitful bough, a fruitful bough by a well;*
> *His branches run over the wall* (Gen. 49:22).

Joseph bore the fruit of a blameless life. He was a benediction to all those with whom he came in contact, not only to his own Jewish family but also to those in the court of Pharaoh. In fact, he provided bread for many who made their way to Egypt during this time of famine. Thus his branches draped over the wall that separated Jews and Gentiles.

So it is that blessings abound wherever the Lord Jesus is found. Although He came primarily to the lost sheep of the house of Israel, He also came *"that the Gentiles might glorify God for His mercy"* (Rom. 15:9). He broke down the middle wall of partition separating the two, thus making peace (Eph. 2:14-22).

In John 4 we have the story of the Lord Jesus speaking to the Samaritan woman at the well of Shechem. Jesus tells her that the blessing of fellowship with God would not be limited to the Jews who worshiped in Jerusalem (Jn. 4:21-24). It would come—in fact was now available—to people like her, people on the other side of the wall. John seems to be reminding us of this connection between Jesus and Joseph when he points out the setting for this story:

> *Then He came to a city of Samaria which is called Sychar, near the plot of ground that Jacob gave to his son Joseph. Now Jacob's well was there. Jesus therefore, being wearied from His journey, sat thus by the well...* (Jn. 4:5-6).

Jacob's blessing of Joseph continues:

> *The archers have bitterly grieved him,*
> *Shot at him and hated him* (Gen. 49:23).

The archers here refer to Joseph's brothers and possibly also to Potiphar's wife who grieved him, mistreated him, and despised him. The language is poetic imagery.

It is not difficult to see the parallel in the life of the Savior. He endured a great contradiction of sinners against Himself. He was assaulted time and again, and hated by those who should have loved Him.

But his bow remained in strength,
And the arms of his hands were made strong
By the hands of the Mighty God of Jacob
(From there is the Shepherd, the Stone of Israel) (Gen. 49:24).

The reference to *"his bow"* continues the thought of the archers from the preceding verse. His bow, however, was not an offensive weapon. It was the strength with which the mighty God of Jacob sustained him. Again the language is poetic and figurative.

The next expression *("From there is the Shepherd, the Stone of Israel")* refers to the Messiah. It seems to say that Christ would be descended from Joseph. But He was descended from Judah. There are two possible explanations. It may mean that the Shepherd comes from the mighty God of Jacob. Or it may mean that the experiences Joseph went through were a foreshadowing of the Messiah's life on earth.

By the God of your father who will help you,
And by the Almighty who will bless you
With blessings of heaven above,
Blessings of the deep that lies beneath,
Blessings of the breasts and of the womb (Gen. 49:25).

The names of God in this passage are magnificent: the mighty God of Jacob, the God of your father, the Almighty. He is the one who would bless Joseph with

- Blessings of heaven above—rain;
- Blessings of the deep that lies beneath—springs, wells, underground reserves of water;

- Blessings of the breasts and of the womb—large families.

This makes us think of the honors that have come to the Lord Jesus as a result of His great redemption: He has the Name that is above every name; He is the Firstborn from the dead; God has made Him both Lord and Christ.

The blessings of your father
Have excelled the blessings of my ancestors,
Up to the utmost bound of the everlasting hills.
They shall be on the head of Joseph,
And on the crown of the head of him
    who was separate from his brothers (Gen. 49:26).

The material blessings that Jacob pronounced on Joseph exceeded the blessings that God had pronounced on his forebears. His inheritance included more territory than any of the brothers received. *"Up to the utmost bound of the everlasting hills"* is poetic language meaning "far reaching." All Joseph's blessings are related to what he endured when he was separated from his brothers, both in character and in geography (Egypt/Canaan).

He inherited the birthright when Reuben forfeited it because he sinned by defiling his father's bed.

Now the sons of Reuben the firstborn of Israel—he was indeed the firstborn, but because he defiled his father's bed, his birthright was given to the sons of Joseph, the son of Israel so that the genealogy is not listed according to the birthright; yet Judah prevailed over his brothers, and from him came a ruler, although the birthright was Joseph's— (1 Chron. 5:1-2).

This means that Joseph would receive a double portion of land. Since his two sons, Ephraim and Manasseh, each received an allotment in Canaan, his tribe did receive the double portion of the firstborn. The genealogy is not listed according to birthright. Ordinarily Reuben would have first place, the primogeniture. But because of Reuben's sin, Joseph inherited the firstborn's portion as far as land is concerned. Judah, on the other hand, received the firstborn's inheritance as far as rule concerned. Through him came a ruler, David. And through David came the ultimate Ruler, the Lord Jesus.

Moving forward to our Redeemer, God has decreed that in all things He shall have the preeminence. His kingdom shall "spread from shore to shore till moons shall wax and wane no more" (*Isaac Watts*).

Chapter Ten

CLOSING SCENES

No vengeance (Gen. 50:15-21)

When Jacob died, the brothers feared that Joseph would get even with them for the way they had treated him. They completely misread his intentions. Joseph had no thought of retaliating. Vengeance belonged to the Lord, not to him (Heb. 10:30). If they knew how much Joseph loved them, they would not have feared.

There is a parallel with our Lord. The Jewish people had cried, *"His blood be upon us and on our children."* Collaborating with the Gentiles, they succeeded in hurrying Him on to His execution. Three days later, when He rose from the tomb, they might have feared revenge. Instead of that, on the Day of Pentecost, the Lord sent His Holy Spirit to Jerusalem, the same city where He had been crucified. The rest of the Book of Acts reveals the Spirit lingering in long-suffering mercy over God's ancient people.

The trembling sinner feareth that God can ne'er forget,
But Christ's full payment cleareth His mem'ry of all debt.
When naught beside could free us or set our souls at large,
Thy holy work, Lord Jesus, secured a full discharge.

—*Mary Bowley Peters*

John's words are pertinent here.

There is no fear in love; but perfect love casts out fear, because fear involves torment. But he who fears has not been made perfect in love (1 Jn. 4:18).

It is the Lord's love for us that casts out our fear. A believer who fears is not appropriating His love. In that sense, he has not been made perfect in love.

In retracing all the sorrow and suffering he had endured, Joseph could see that God was working out His purposes through it all. The Lord allowed man to have his wickedness but He had His way. He was making the wrath of men to praise Him (Ps. 76:10). So Joseph comforted his brothers. He was not in the place of God to take vengeance on them (Gen. 50:19). Although they had intended to murder him, God overruled and brought out a happy ending.

But as for you, you meant evil against me; but God meant it for good, in order to bring it about as it is this day, to save many people alive (Gen. 50:20).

In his book, *The Cross in Christian Experience,* W. M. Clow measures the greatness of Joseph's character:

There is no act in any drama to match in tender feeling, and in exalted motive, Joseph's forgiveness of his brothers. Their sin had been murder. They had kept the real truth locked up in their hearts, heedless of what came of their brother. They had given Jacob twenty years of sorrow. They did Joseph that crowning injustice of mistrusting him after he had given them ample evidence of his kindly feeling. In that last scene, where they came bowing down to him in fear lest now he should seek his revenge, Joseph reveals his God-likeness. He does not dismiss them with an assurance that bygones are bygones, and a caustic counsel not to think evil. He meets them with the quick and tender words of a reconciled love, which sweeps the last trace of fear out of their hearts, and binds them to him in an endearing affection. That is how God forgives.[13]

Joseph's greathearted words find echoes in the experience of our Lord. In his historic message on the day of Pentecost, Peter said,

Him, being delivered by the determined purpose and foreknowledge of God, you have taken by lawless hands, have crucified, and put to death (Acts 2:23).

The men of Israel had succeeded in putting Jesus of Nazareth to death, but it happened by the determined counsel and foreknowledge of God. What was intended for evil turned out for good. God raised up Jesus and made Him Lord and Christ (Acts 2:36). Now the good news of salvation goes out to the people of Israel, to their children, and to as many as the Lord calls (Acts 2:39). The mob had intended the destruction of Jesus, but God meant it for their salvation. He worked everything together for good.

One who cares (Gen. 50:21)

With comforting words, Joseph, the exalted son of Jacob promised his brothers that he would care for them.

Just so, the exalted Son of God promises His own that He will save, keep, and satisfy them. They will never hunger or thirst and He will never leave nor forsake them (Heb. 13:5). We can cast all our care on Him, knowing that He cares for us (1 Pet. 5:7).

The death of Joseph (Gen. 50:26)

An unknown psalmist gives a cameo of Joseph's life:

> *Moreover He called for a famine in the land;*
> *He destroyed all the provision of bread.*
> *He sent a man before them—Joseph—who was sold as a slave.*
> *They hurt his feet with fetters;*
> *He was laid in irons.*
> *Until the time that His word came to pass,*
> *The word of the Lord tested him.*
> *The king sent and released him;*
> *The ruler of the people let him go free.*
> *He made him lord of his house,*
> *And ruler of all his possessions,*
> *To bind his princes at his pleasure,*
> *And teach his elders wisdom.*
> *Israel also came into Egypt,*
> *And Jacob dwelt in the land of Ham* (Ps. 105:16-23).

Joseph was 110 when he died. They embalmed his body, placed it in a coffin in Egypt, and carried it to Canaan.

The "Greater than Joseph" not only died and was anointed; He rose from the dead, never to die again, and ascended to the heavenly Canaan.[14] Joseph's body too will rise, be reunited with his spirit, and be glorified forever, just like his Antitype.

A pilgrim and stranger (Gen. 50:24-25)

Just before he died, Joseph said to his brothers, *"I am dying; but God will surely visit you, and bring you out of this land."* Spurgeon's comment on this is notable:

> Joseph had been an incarnate providence, a heaven-sent protector, to his brethren. When [he] died, a thousand comforts died with him. But see how that pain was soothed! The survivors had a promise that the living God would visit them. A visit from God! What a favor! What a consolation! What a heaven below! Lord, visit us this day, although indeed we are not worthy that Thou shouldest come under our roof.

Just before He died, the Lord Jesus said, *"I go to My Father, and you see Me no more"* (Jn. 16:10). But He would not leave them orphans (Jn. 14:18). He would send the Holy Spirit to be with them forever and He Himself would be with them, even to the end of the age.

One of the last mentions of Joseph in the Bible is in Hebrews 11:22.

> *By faith Joseph, when he was dying, made mention of the departure of the children of Israel, and gave instructions concerning his bones.*

He obviously knew of God's covenant with Abram, and how He had said:

Know certainly that your descendants will be strangers in a land that is not theirs, and will serve them, and they will afflict them four hundred years. And also the nation whom they serve will I judge; afterward they shall come out with great possessions (Gen. 15:13-14).

Joseph did not live to see the departure of the children of Israel from Egypt, but by faith he saw the invisible and made the future present.

The instruction concerning his bones opens his heart to us. He had lived most of his life in Egypt. He had served well in the royal palace. In a time of great famine, he preserved the lives of multitudes. That country held many wonderful memories for him. But Egypt was not the homeland of his soul. Although his body was there, his heart was in Canaan. If he couldn't get home, he wanted his bones to be there.

Maclaren says,

He filled his place at Pharaoh's court, but his dying words open a window into his soul, and betray how little he had felt that he belonged to the order of things in the midst of which he had been content to live. Though surrounded by an ancient civilization; and dwelling among granite temples and solid pyramids and firm-based sphinxes, the very emblems of eternity; he confessed that he had here no continuing city, but sought one to come.[15]

Chapter Eleven

MOSES' FINAL TRIBUTE

As we conclude our study of the life of Joseph, we must go back to the blessing that Moses pronounced on this one who speaks to us so eloquently of the Lord Jesus.

Moses' blessing on Joseph (Deut. 33:13-17).

Moses gave Joseph the longest blessing of all the sons of Jacob. Of Joseph he said:

> *Blessed of the Lord is his land,*
> *With the precious things of heaven, with the dew,*
> *And the deep lying beneath* (Deut. 33:13).

Joseph's tribal allotment would be the best part of the land. It would enjoy abundance of rain, dew, springs, wells, and an underground water table.

> *With the precious fruits of the sun,*
> *With the precious produce of the months* (Deut. 33:14).

The land would produce luxuriant crops of fruit and vegetables, thanks to the photosynthesizing action of the sun and the regularity of the lunar months.

With the best things of the ancient mountains,
With the precious things of the everlasting hills (Deut. 33:15).

The mountains and hills would be clothed in rich stands of timber, important for producing oxygen and for building materials and fuel.

With the precious things of the earth and its fullness,
And the favor of Him who dwelt in the bush.
Let the blessing come on the head of Joseph,
And on the crown of the head of him who was separate from his brothers (Deut. 33:16).

The precious things of the earth and its fullness may refer to bumper crops, but since these are already promised in verse 14, the reference may be to mineral deposits.

Joseph's blessing indicates special favor from the Angel of the Lord who appeared to Moses *"in a flame of fire in the midst of a bush"* (Ex. 3:2). The Angel of the Lord was Christ in a pre-incarnate appearance.

Moses' blessing was prophetic. All these benefits would come to Joseph, who was separate from his brothers from the time they sold him to the Midianites to their reunion in the court of Pharaoh.

His glory is like a firstborn bull,
And his horns like the horns of the wild ox;

Together with them
He shall push the peoples
To the ends of the earth;
They are the ten thousands of Ephraim,
And they are the thousands of Manasseh (Deut. 33:17).

Joseph would also enjoy military triumphs as the armies of his sons, Ephraim and Manasseh, like bulls and oxen, would push their enemies to the end of the Bible land.

The preeminence which Jacob gave to Ephraim over Manasseh (Gen. 48:14ff) is seen here in that Ephraim had ten thousands whereas his brother had only a few thousand.

Chapter Twelve

STEPHEN'S REFERENCE TO JOSEPH

When the martyr Stephen was called to make his defense, he gave the following pointed reference to Joseph:

And the patriarchs, becoming envious, sold Joseph into Egypt. But God was with him and delivered him out of all his troubles, and gave him favor and wisdom in the presence of Pharaoh, king of Egypt; and he made him governor over Egypt and all his house. Now a famine and great trouble came over all the land of Egypt and Canaan. And our fathers found no sustenance.

But when Jacob heard that there was grain in Egypt, he sent out our fathers first. And the second time Joseph was made known to his brothers, and Joseph's family became known to the Pharaoh. Then Joseph came and called his father Jacob and all his relatives to him, seventy-five people. So Jacob went down to Egypt; and he died, he and our fathers. And they were carried back to Shechem and laid in the tomb that Abraham bought for a sum of money from the sons of Hamor, the father of Shechem (Acts 7:9-16).

Stephen's antagonists had accused him of speaking blasphemous words against the temple and the law of Moses (Acts 6:13). In fact, he was alleged to say that Jesus would destroy the temple and change the customs that Moses taught (Acts 6:14). In his answer, he said that it was characteristic of Israel to reject leaders whom God raised up and to resist changes which the Lord instituted. Here are his stinging words:

> You stiff-necked and uncircumcised in heart and ears! You always resist the Holy Spirit; as your fathers did, so do you. Which of the prophets did your fathers not persecute? And they killed those who foretold the coming of the Just One, of whom you have become the betrayers and murderers, who have received the law by the direction of angels and have not kept it (Acts 7:51-53).

In other words, the way Joseph's brothers had treated him was a picture of the way Israel treated the leaders God had appointed and ultimately the Lord Jesus.

For this fearless indictment Stephen paid with his life.

Chapter Thirteen

LESSONS FROM THE LIFE OF JOSEPH

Before we close the book on the life of Joseph, let us review some of the lessons we learn from that life.

• Sometimes the best people are least appreciated. Jesus said that a great person gets more honor from the general public than he does from his own family (Mt. 13:57).

• Bad things sometimes happen to good people. Believers are not immune to sickness, sorrow, tragedy, persecution, and other ills that plague mankind. But their sufferings are limited to this life. And God harnesses these experiences as part of our education. If our lives were all sunshine, they would be a desert. Trials don't seem pleasant at the time but afterward they yield the peaceable fruit of righteousness to those who have been trained by them (Heb. 12:11).

• Man has his wickedness but God has His way. The Lord allows Satan a certain length of leash, but then He overrules the wickedness for His glory and the blessing of the saints.

• For the child of God nothing happens in life by chance. Luck and fortune are not words in the Christian vocabulary. What seems to be accidental is actually part of a divine weaving.

• The way of the transgressor is hard. Joseph's brothers thought they had succeeded in their diabolical plot, but their consciences would not be silenced until finally they went through great tribulation and were exposed. I am reminded of a man who said, "I don't know much about the Bible but I do know that the way of the transgressor is hard."

• Be sure your sin will find you out. You can't sin and get away with it. Payday is sure to come, either in this life or in the next. In *The Dream of Eugene Aram,* a fellow by that name murdered a man and cast his body in the river, "a sluggish water, black as ink, the depth was so extreme." The next morning he revisited the scene:

> And sought the black accursed pool,
> With a wild, misgiving eye;
> And he saw the dead in the river bed,
> For the faithless stream was dry.

He quickly covered the corpse with loads of leaves, but a great wind swept through the woods and left the secret exposed to the elements.

> Then down I cast me on my face,
> And first began to weep,
> For I knew my secret then was one
> That earth refused to keep,
> On land or sea, though it should be
> Ten thousand fathoms deep.

Finally, he took the body to a cave and covered it with heaps of stones, but after years had passed, the murder was discovered and Eugene Aram was executed.

• We reap what we sow. If we sow to the flesh, we will of the flesh reap corruption. If we sow to the Spirit we will of the Spirit reap everlasting life (Gal. 6:8).

• God honors those who honor Him. It is a law of life. It is written, *"Those who honor Me I will honor"* (1 Sam. 2:30). Joseph proved it to be true. So did Eric Liddell. In 1924 he refused to run in the Olympics on the Lord's Day. On a weekday he ran in the 400-meter race and set a new world record. He was honored then at home and abroad. Fifty-seven years later a film named *Chariots of Fire* honored Eric Liddell with worldwide acclaim.

• We are all tempted. There is no sin in being tempted. The sin lies in yielding to it. We don't have to sin. We sin only when we want to. There is always a way of escape. *"No temptation has overtaken you except such as is com-*

mon to man; but God is faithful, who will not allow you to be tempted beyond what you are able, but with the temptation will also make a way of escape, that you may be able to bear it" (1 Cor. 10:13). The way of escape is to call on the Lord, like Peter did when he was sinking beneath the waves (Mt. 14:30). *"The name of the Lord is a strong tower; the righteous run to it and are safe"* (Prov. 18:10).

• Sometimes escape from temptation requires strong, resolute action on our part. Jesus taught that when He said, *"If your hand makes you sin, cut it off...If your foot makes you sin, cut it off...If your eye makes you sin, pluck it out"* (Mk. 9:43, 45, 47).

• When tempted by Potiphar's wife, Joseph said, "How can I do this great wickedness and sin against God." In other words, he lived with the consciousness of being in the line of vision of an all-seeing God. A customer asked Adam Clarke to make a dishonest sale, saying, "Go ahead. Your boss is not looking." Clarke replied, "My Boss is always looking."

• Another factor that influenced Joseph when tempted was that he would have been unfaithful to his earthly master if he had sinned with his master's wife. We should be faithful to our masters according to the flesh, *"not with eyeservice, as men-pleasers, but as servants of Christ, doing the will of God from the heart"* (Eph. 6:5-8).

• In resisting a temptation, we might lose a coat but we'll gain a crown. A coat can be easily replaced; a character can't. There is a cost to being a true believer, but the gains far outweigh the losses. The losses are temporal; the gains are eternal.

• God is pleased when we suffer for doing good but not when we deserve to suffer. Suffering for righteousness sake marks us out as distinctly Christian. It says that we are a cut above the world.

• We should not wait till circumstances are ideal before we get to work for the Lord. *"He who observes the wind will not sow, and he who regards the clouds will not reap"* (Eccl. 11:4). Circumstances are seldom perfect. Even in prison Joseph busied himself in service to others.

• We should not grow weary in well doing. We shall reap if we don't faint (Gal. 6:9). It takes time for grain to ripen and for harvest to come. So it is in the spiritual realm. Don't look for quick results.

• The way of blessing is to acknowledge our sins promptly and obtain forgiveness. Think of the misery the brothers of Joseph could have saved themselves if they had confessed their sins earlier. But no! They stubbornly refused to break until they were severely tested and tried. Joseph put them through experiences that made them remember in detail how they had treated him.

• We have been forgiven millions; we should forgive for a few pennies (see Mt. 18:21-25). Joseph's forgiveness pictures how the Lord forgives us when we confess our sins. We don't have to ask Him to forgive. All we have to do is confess. He does the rest.

• Every knee must bow. Picture Potiphar's wife bowing before Joseph. And Potiphar himself. And the Egyptians, who despised the Hebrews. Every knee will one day bow to the Lord Jesus. Hitler, Stalin, and Chairman Mao will bow. Every knee. It is better to bow now voluntarily than later by compulsion at the Judgment of the Great White Throne.

• We should show grace to our brothers and sisters in Christ. No matter how irritating some of them may be to us at times, they are dear to God. The precious blood of Christ has redeemed them. We should try to see the Lord Jesus in them.

• Gratitude for salvation should lead to total consecration. Joseph's deliverance of his family was from material, temporal famine. Yet they said, *"We will be your servants."* By His death Christ has delivered us from sin, death, and eternal hell. The only proper response is to say, "You have bled and died for me. Henceforth I will live for Thee."

• The secret of Joseph's life is that the Lord was with him. In one sense, He is with all His people. But He was with Joseph in the sense of intimate fellowship. Joseph's life of faith and obedience endeared him to the Lord in a special way. As a result, God blessed him with success.

• The way up is down. This is preeminently seen in the life of the Lord Jesus (Phil. 2:5-11). He went down to Bethlehem, Gabbatha, Gethsemane, and Calvary. There He became obedient unto death, even the death of the cross. Now God has highly exalted Him, given Him the superlative name, and honored Him with universal dominion. We see it in the life of Joseph—down to the pit and the prison, then up to the palace. It can be true in our lives also. If we humble ourselves under the mighty hand of God, He will exalt us in due time (1 Pet. 5:6).

> If you want to be high, stoop low;
> If you want to go up, go down;
> But go as low as e'er you will,
> The Savior has gone lower still.

• We can't always trace God's hand but we can always trust His heart (*Spurgeon*). His judgments are often unsearchable, and His ways past finding out. His way is in the sea, and His path in the great waters, and His footsteps are not known (Ps. 77:19). But we can be confident that everything that comes into our life is filtered through His wisdom and love.

• Lifetime is training time for reigning time. The Lord has given each one of us both gifts and the ability to exercise those gifts (Mt. 25:14-30; Lk. 19:13-27). The extent to which we are faithful in using them determines the breadth of our rule in the millennial kingdom.

• Deceit often backfires. The brothers had told their father that a wild animal had probably killed Joseph. Later they had to admit that it was a lie. Sir Walter Scott was right when he said, "O what a tangled web we weave when first we practice to deceive."

127

- If you are falsely accused or slandered, as Joseph was, you don't have to defend yourself. Leave it with the Lord and He will vindicate you. *"The battle is not yours, but God's"* (2 Chron. 20:15).

> *No weapon formed against you shall prosper,*
> *And every tongue which rises against you in judgment*
> *You shall condemn.*
> *This is the heritage of the servants of the Lord,*
> *And their righteousness is from Me,*
> *Says the Lord* (Isa. 54:17).

- Cream rises to the surface. In this connection, Joseph reminds us of Proverbs 22:29:

> *Do you see a man who excels in his work? He will stand before kings. He will not stand before unknown men.*

- A father often sees his scandalous behavior reproduced in the life of his son. Jacob was a cheat. So were some of his sons. This is sin's scorpion sting. There is a sense in which the Lord still visits the sins of the fathers on the third and fourth generation (Ex. 34:7).

- It is interesting to see how Jacob sent all kinds of money and produce to pay for the grain that he needed. The parallel today is that men would rather pay for salvation than receive it as a free gift. Joseph had no intention of charging his brothers for their food. He wanted that food to be a gift of grace. Paul elaborates on this in Romans 4:4-5:

> *Now to him who works, the wages are not counted as grace but as*

*debt. But to him who does not work but believes on Him who jus-
tifies the ungodly, his faith is accounted for righteousness.*

• Joseph said, *"You meant evil against me; but God
meant it for good"* (Gen. 50:20). Here you have the curious mingling of the human and the divine. Man proposes
but God disposes. Our sovereign God has the last word.
And for His people, the last word is always good. The
Apostle Paul said, *"All things work together for good to
those who love God, to those who are the called according to His purpose"* (Rom. 8:28). Everything is geared to
conform us to the image of His Son, and what could be
better than that?

• William Cowper's hymn could have been written with
Joseph's experiences in view. In fact, it is difficult to read
the story of Joseph without thinking of these lines:

God moves in a mysterious way His wonders to perform;
He plants His footsteps in the sea and rides upon the storm.

Ye fearful saints, fresh courage take; the clouds ye so much dread
Are big with mercy, and shall break in blessings on your head.

Judge not the Lord by feeble sense, but trust Him for His grace;
Behind a frowning providence He hides a smiling face.

His purposes will ripen fast, unfolding every hour;
The bud may have a bitter taste, but sweet will be the flower.

Blind unbelief is sure to err, and scan His work in vain:
God is His own interpreter, and He will make it plain.

• Joseph lived long before the Christian era. He had no

Bible and no Christian teaching. Yet his life would compare favorably with committed Christians today. He used what knowledge of the Lord he had, and made the most of it.

• A life that's lived for God has a lasting ministry. Joseph is home in heaven, but he still speaks to us. If he had not been a man of character who put the Lord first in his life, he would be unknown in the obscurity of Egyptian mummies. In that connection, Spurgeon said,

> A good character is the best tombstone. Those who loved you and were helped by you will remember you when forget-me-nots are withered. Carve your name on hearts, and not on marble.

• At times it seemed that everything was against Joseph, but he was on the winning side.

> O changeless sea, thy message
> In changing spray is cast.
> Within God's plan of progress
> It matters not at last
> How wide the shores of evil,
> How strong the reefs of sin,
> The wave may be defeated
> But the tide is sure to win.
> —*Priscilla Leonard*

• Joseph is a good example of endurance. He didn't give up easily. His life was mostly routine, humdrum work. The mountaintop experiences were the exception. He was content to press on, filling each day with productive labor. He reminds us of William Carey, who said, "I am not a great preacher, but I can plod."

Sometimes Joseph is cited to show that Christians should engage in politics. It is a mistake. Joseph was not a politician. He did not run for office. He was a civil servant.

First Peter 2:12 is eminently appropriate when applied to Joseph:

> Having your conduct honorable among the Gentiles, that when they speak against you as evildoers, they may by your good works which they observe, glorify God in the day of visitation.

Chapter Fourteen

SUMMARY

God raised up Joseph, as no other, to be a type of His beloved Son. It is impossible to ponder the character and experiences of this son of Jacob without thinking of Jesus. Although Joseph was an imperfect type, as all types are, the similarities are inescapable.

Joseph was a man of integrity and principle, an example of moral greatness. His many resolutions brought him through the fires of temptation so that we remember him for his purity. He wore the white flower of a blameless life.

His was a kindly disposition, tender, affectionate, and sympathetic. For one who had no Bible and no permanently indwelling Holy Spirit, we would not expect to see such a display of the fruit of the Spirit: love, joy, peace, longsuffering, kindness, goodness, faithfulness, gentleness, and self-control.

On one hand we see his endurance in suffering, on the other his grace, mercy, and forgiveness to his adversaries. We admire his wisdom and skill in administering the affairs of a great nation. It seems that there were no problems he could not solve. He was capable, dependable, and faithful. Through it all he was modest, selfless, and humble, determined not to touch the glory that belonged to God alone. His faith enabled him to see the invisible and make the future present.

We will see Joseph again. When the trumpet sounds and we are taken to our Promised Land, he will be there, resplendent in glory, testifying to the sovereign grace of God.

ENDNOTES

1 A type is a person, event, or object in the Old Testament that resembles someone or something in the New. A type has likeness or similarity. It foreshadows, pre-pictures, represents, or illustrates. Joseph is a type of Jesus because there are so many ways in which he resembles our Lord.

2 In Daniel 7:9-10, the Ancient of Days is the Lord Jesus. We know this by comparing these verses with Revelation 1:13-15. In Daniel 7:13, the Ancient of Days is God the Father.

3 Christopher Knapp, *A Fruitful Bough,* Neptune, NJ: Loizeaux Bros., Inc, n.d., pp. 18-23.

4 The Law of Moses required Him to answer or be judged guilty (Lev. 5:1).

5 F. B. Meyer, *Through the Bible Day by Day,* Philadelphia: American Sunday School Union, 1914, pp. 47-48.

6 This is poetic license. Jesus was not buried in a cave but in a tomb hewn from the rock.

7 C. A. Coates, *An Outline of the Book of Genesis,* Sussex, England: Kingston Bible Trust, n.d., p. 228.

8 F. B. Meyer, *Joseph, Beloved, Hated, Exalted,* Fort Washington, PA: Christian Literature Crusade, 1960, p. 63.

9 Christopher Knapp, *A Fruitful Bough,* Neptune, NJ; Loizeaux Bros., Inc. n.d., pp. 75-76.

10 John J. Davis, *Paradise to Prison,* Winona Lake, IN: BMH Books, 1975, p. 278.

11 C. R. Erdman, *The Book of Genesis,* New York: Fleming H. Revell Company, 1950, p. 122.

12 F. B. Meyer, *Joseph, Beloved, Hated, Exalted,* Fort Washington, PA: Christian Literature Crusade, 1960, p. 98.

13 W. M. Clow, *The Cross in Christian Experience,* New York: George Doran, 1908, p. 274.

14 The land of Canaan is often a picture not of heaven but of the present place of the believer's conflict, victory, and blessings. The book of Ephesians calls this *"the heavenlies."* However, Canaan can also sometimes be a picture of heaven itself where our Joshua gives us rest from our enemies, where our David rules, where our Melchizedek is ever living to intercede for us.

15 Alexander Maclaren, *Expositions of Holy Scripture, Vol. 1,* Grand Rapids, MI: Baker Book House, 1974, p. 319.

SCRIPTURE INDEX

49:24-25	105		5:1, 2	13
49:26	106			
50:1	73, 101		2 CHRONICLES	
50:7-14	95		20:15	128
50:13-14	102			
50:15-21	109		PSALMS	
50:17	73		2:8	49
50:18	15		22:16	48
50:19	110		22:27	51
50:20	110, 129		20-21	24
50:21	112		40:1-2	22
50:24-25	113		41:9	24
50:26	112		45:2	40
			55:12-14	24
EXODUS			69:8	14
21:5	36		76:10	110
21:32	25		77:19	127
3:2	116		105:18	47
34:7	128		105:16-23	112
			105:19	48
LEVITICUS			110:3	15
5:1	135			
			PROVERBS	
NUMBERS			18:10	124
23:9	99		22:29	128
			26:7	31
DEUTERONOMY				
15:18	36		ECCLESIASTES	
18:10-11	75		11:4	125
33:13-17	115			
33:15-16	116		ISAIAH	
33:17	117		6:9-10	66
			8:18	59
1 SAMUEL			9:6	50
2:30	123		9:6	51
			30:18	72
1 CHRONICLES			44:21	47
5:1-2	106		45:23	52